Unlocking LinkedIn's Potential:

A Beginner's Guide to Success

Nick O. Walter

TABLE OF CONTENTS

CHAPTER 6: HARNESSING THE POWER OF LINKEDIN ANALYTICS

6.1 Tracking profile views and engagement

6.2 Analyzing post-performance and audience insights

6.3 Using data to optimize your LinkedIn strategy

CHAPTER 7: ADVANCED LINKEDIN STRATEGIES

7.1 Building a personal brand on LinkedIn

7.2 Leveraging LinkedIn for thought leadership

7.3 Exploring LinkedIn advertising options

7.4 Networking techniques for career growth

7.5 Leveraging LinkedIn for business and entrepreneurship

CHAPTER 8: MAINTAINING A PROFESSIONAL ONLINE PRESENCE

8.1 Managing privacy settings

8.2 Handling endorsements and recommendations

8.3 Dealing with negative feedback or criticism

INTRODUCTION

Are you ready to unlock the untapped potential of LinkedIn and propel your professional success to new heights? Look no further! "Unlocking LinkedIn's Potential: A Beginner's Guide to Success" is your passport to mastering the world's premier professional networking platform.

In today's hyper-connected world, LinkedIn has emerged as the go-to platform for professionals seeking career growth, networking opportunities, and industry insights. However, navigating the intricacies of LinkedIn can be daunting, especially for beginners. That's where this book comes in, serving as your trusted companion on the journey to LinkedIn mastery.

Imagine a world where you effortlessly attract job offers, connect with influential industry leaders, and showcase your skills to a global audience hungry for talent. With "Unlocking LinkedIn's Potential," that world is within your grasp. We'll demystify the secrets, strategies, and tactics that will transform your LinkedIn presence from mediocre to magnetic.

Whether you're a recent graduate eager to land your dream job, a seasoned professional looking to expand your network, or an aspiring thought leader seeking to establish your personal brand, this book is tailored to meet your needs. We'll take you step-by-step through the process of setting up an attention-grabbing profile, building a powerful network, leveraging LinkedIn's features, and engaging effectively with your audience.

But this book isn't just about the basics. We'll delve into advanced strategies that will elevate you above the competition, from crafting a compelling personal brand to harnessing LinkedIn analytics for data-driven decision making. You'll learn how to navigate the ever-evolving LinkedIn landscape with finesse, staying ahead of the curve and seizing every opportunity that comes your way.

Prepare to be captivated by real-life success stories, inspired by industry experts who have harnessed the full potential of LinkedIn, and equipped with practical tips and techniques that you can implement immediately. Get ready to open doors, forge valuable connections, and unlock a world of professional opportunities that were once beyond your reach.

Now is the time to take control of your LinkedIn journey. "Unlocking LinkedIn's Potential" is your key to unlocking a future filled with endless possibilities. So, fasten your seatbelt, embark on this exhilarating LinkedIn adventure, and get ready to unleash your true professional potential like never before. The world is waiting for you, and LinkedIn is your gateway to success. Let's dive in!

Chapter 1: Introduction to LinkedIn

1.1 What is LinkedIn?

LinkedIn is a professional networking platform that connects individuals and businesses worldwide. It serves as a virtual hub for professionals to establish their online presence, showcase their skills and experiences, and connect with like-minded individuals in their industry.

At its core, LinkedIn is designed to facilitate professional connections and opportunities. It allows users to create a detailed profile that acts as a digital resume, highlighting their education, work experience, skills, certifications, and accomplishments. Users can also upload a professional profile picture and write a compelling summary to introduce themselves to potential connections.

One of the key features of LinkedIn is its emphasis on building a network of professional connections. Users can connect with colleagues, classmates, industry peers, and even influential figures in their field. These connections can open doors to new career opportunities, collaborations, mentorship, and industry insights. Users can also join industry-specific groups and participate in discussions, further expanding their professional network.

LinkedIn serves as a powerful platform for job seekers and recruiters alike. Job seekers can search and apply for jobs directly on the platform, as well as receive job recommendations based on their profile and interests.

LinkedIn also offers premium features such as InMail, which enables users to send direct messages to professionals outside of their immediate network, making it easier to connect with potential employers or clients.

Companies and organizations can create their own LinkedIn pages to establish a professional presence and engage with their target audience. These pages can showcase company updates, job openings, and relevant industry content. LinkedIn also offers advertising options, allowing businesses to promote their products, services, and job postings to a highly targeted audience.

Furthermore, LinkedIn provides a wealth of resources for professional development. Users can access educational content, industry news, and thought leadership articles shared by industry experts and influencers. LinkedIn Learning, a subsidiary of LinkedIn, offers a wide range of online courses and tutorials to help users acquire new skills and enhance their professional knowledge.

Overall, LinkedIn is a comprehensive professional networking platform that enables individuals and businesses to connect, collaborate, and grow their professional networks. It serves as a hub for career development, job searching, and industry insights, making it an essential tool for professionals in virtually every field.

1.2 Why is LinkedIn important for professionals?

LinkedIn is an essential platform for professionals due to its numerous benefits and significance in the modern business landscape. Here are several key reasons why LinkedIn is important for professionals:

★ **Networking opportunities**: LinkedIn provides a powerful networking platform where professionals can connect with colleagues, industry peers, potential employers, and clients. Building and nurturing professional relationships is crucial for career advancement, business opportunities, and gaining industry insights.

★ **Professional branding**: LinkedIn allows professionals to establish and enhance their personal brand. Users can create a compelling profile showcasing their skills, experience, and achievements. It serves as an online resume that can be easily shared with others, including recruiters and hiring managers.

★ **Job search and recruitment**: LinkedIn has become a go-to platform for job seekers and recruiters alike. Professionals can actively search for job opportunities, apply directly through the platform, and receive relevant job recommendations based on their skills and preferences. Employers and recruiters use LinkedIn to find and evaluate potential candidates, leveraging the platform's vast talent pool.

★ **Industry knowledge and insights**: LinkedIn provides access to a wealth of industry-specific content, discussions, and thought leadership articles shared by professionals worldwide. By engaging in relevant groups, following influencers, and participating in conversations, professionals can stay updated on the latest trends, industry news, and insights, fostering professional growth and learning.

★ **Business development and lead generation**: LinkedIn offers opportunities for professionals to generate leads, establish partnerships, and explore new business prospects. Users can leverage the platform's advanced search filters to identify potential clients, collaborators, or investors. LinkedIn also enables professionals to share valuable content, showcase their expertise, and engage with a broader audience, thus attracting potential business opportunities.

★ **Professional community and collaboration**: LinkedIn foster a sense of community among professionals, connecting individuals with like-minded peers, industry groups, and alumni networks. Users can join and participate in relevant discussions, seek advice, share knowledge, and collaborate on projects. These interactions can lead to valuable connections, mentorship opportunities, and partnerships.

★ **Industry reputation and credibility**: Active engagement and participation on LinkedIn can contribute to establishing professional credibility and thought leadership. By sharing insightful content, participating in discussions, and receiving endorsements or recommendations, professionals can enhance their reputation within their industry and gain credibility among their peers and potential clients or employers.

★ **Continuous learning and skill development**: LinkedIn Learning, an integrated feature of the platform, offers a vast library of online courses and tutorials covering various professional skills and subjects. Professionals can access these resources to upskill, acquire new knowledge, and stay competitive in a rapidly evolving job market.

Overall, LinkedIn is important for professionals because it facilitates networking, personal branding, job search, recruitment, industry knowledge sharing, business development, community engagement, and skill development. Leveraging LinkedIn's features and opportunities can significantly enhance professional growth, career prospects, and industry influence.

1.3 Benefits of using LinkedIn for beginners

LinkedIn is a powerful platform that offers numerous benefits for beginners and professionals alike. Here are some of the key advantages of using LinkedIn for beginners:

★ **Professional Networking**: LinkedIn provides an excellent opportunity to build and expand your professional network. You can connect with colleagues, classmates, mentors, industry experts, and potential employers. Networking on LinkedIn can lead to new job opportunities, partnerships, and valuable connections within your industry.

★ **Job Search**: LinkedIn is a valuable resource for job seekers. You can create a comprehensive profile that showcases your skills, experiences, and accomplishments. Recruiters and hiring managers actively search for candidates on LinkedIn, and having a strong presence increases your chances of being discovered. Additionally, LinkedIn's job board allows you to search and apply for relevant positions directly on the platform.

★ **Personal Branding**: LinkedIn offers a platform to establish and enhance your personal brand. You can create a professional profile that highlights your expertise, achievements, and interests. By sharing relevant content, participating in industry discussions, and engaging with others, you can establish yourself as a thought leader and gain credibility in your field.

★ **Learning and Knowledge Sharing**: LinkedIn is a hub for professional learning and knowledge sharing. You can join industry-specific groups, follow influencers, and participate in discussions to stay updated on the latest trends and insights. LinkedIn also offers various learning resources, including LinkedIn Learning, where you can access a wide range of courses to develop new skills and enhance your professional development.

★ **Business Development and Lead Generation**: For entrepreneurs and business professionals, LinkedIn can be a valuable tool for business development and lead generation. You can identify and connect with potential clients, partners, and suppliers. Additionally, LinkedIn's advanced search filters allow you to target specific industries, job titles, or geographic locations, making it easier to find and engage with your target audience.

★ **Reputation Management**: LinkedIn allows you to manage your professional reputation effectively. You can request recommendations from colleagues and clients, which adds credibility to your profile. Additionally, by actively engaging in conversations and sharing valuable content, you can shape how others perceive you and your expertise.

★

★ **Industry Insights and Trends**: LinkedIn provides a platform to stay informed about industry insights, news, and trends. By following relevant companies, influencers, and industry publications, you can access valuable content and stay up-to-date with the latest developments in your field. This knowledge can help you adapt and make informed decisions to stay competitive in your industry.

★ **Mentorship and Guidance**: LinkedIn offers opportunities for mentorship and guidance. You can connect with experienced professionals in your field who can provide advice, guidance, and support. Engaging with mentors on LinkedIn can help you navigate your career path, gain valuable insights, and access opportunities that may not be readily available.

Overall, LinkedIn offers a wide range of benefits for beginners. By leveraging these advantages, beginners can enhance their professional growth, expand their network, and unlock new career opportunities.

Chapter 2: Setting Up Your LinkedIn Profile

2.1 Creating an Account

Creating an account on LinkedIn is a straightforward process that allows you to establish a professional presence and connect with other professionals in your industry. By following a few simple steps, you can set up your LinkedIn account and begin leveraging the platform for networking, job searching, and career development. Here's a detailed guide to help you create your LinkedIn account:

- **Visit the LinkedIn website**: Open your preferred web browser and go to www.linkedin.com. You can as well download the LinkedIn mobile app from your app store.

- **Sign up**: On the LinkedIn homepage, you will find a sign-up form. Begin by entering your first name, last name, email address, and a password. Make sure to choose a strong password to protect your account.

- **Verify your email**: After submitting the sign-up form, LinkedIn will ask you to confirm your email address. LinkedIn will then send a verification email to the address you provided. Check your inbox and click on the verification link to confirm your email address.

- **Add your location and current position**: Upon email verification, LinkedIn will prompt you to add your location, education and current position. This information helps LinkedIn personalize your experience and connect you with professionals in your area and industry. You can choose to skip this step and add the information later if you prefer.

  You will then be prompted to connect with people you may know by importing your contacts from your email account. You can skip this step if you don't want to connect with your contacts yet.

- **Customize your profile**: To create a compelling LinkedIn profile, click on the "Me" icon in the top right corner and select "View profile." Here, you can add essential details such as your headline (a concise description of your professional identity), a professional profile picture, a background photo, a summary highlighting your skills and experience, education history, work experience, and any relevant certifications or achievements.

- **Optimize your profile**: Enhance your profile's visibility by optimizing it for search engines and LinkedIn's internal search feature. Incorporate relevant keywords throughout your profile to improve your chances of appearing in search results when recruiters or professionals search for individuals with specific skills or experience.

- **Expand your network**: Connect with professionals you know by importing your contacts from your email address book or by manually searching for individuals you want to connect with. LinkedIn also suggests connections based on your industry, education, and work experience.

- **Join relevant groups**: Find and join LinkedIn groups that align with your professional interests and goals. Engaging in group discussions and sharing valuable insights can help you expand your network, establish credibility, and stay updated with industry trends.

- **Explore LinkedIn features**: Familiarize yourself with LinkedIn's features, such as the newsfeed, where you can discover and engage with content relevant to your industry. Additionally, LinkedIn offers features like job search, learning courses, and events that can aid in your professional development. You can also join groups, follow companies, and engage with content by liking, commenting, or sharing.

- **Personalize your LinkedIn URL**: Customize your LinkedIn profile URL to make it more professional and easier to share. Ideally, use your full name or a variation of it in the URL.

- **Review your privacy settings**: LinkedIn provides privacy settings that allow you to control what information is visible to others and who can contact you. Review these settings to ensure your profile's visibility aligns with your preferences.

- **Keep your profile updated**: Regularly update your LinkedIn profile to reflect your latest achievements, work experience, and skills. This will demonstrate your professional growth and keep your connections informed.

That's it! You're now ready to leverage LinkedIn to connect with professionals, showcase your expertise, and explore new career opportunities.

Remember, LinkedIn is a professional networking platform, so maintain a professional tone, engage thoughtfully, and be mindful of the content you share. By creating an informative and engaging LinkedIn profile, actively connecting with professionals, and leveraging the platform's features, you can maximize your presence on LinkedIn and unlock numerous opportunities for career advancement and professional growth.

2.2 Choosing the Right Profile Picture

Choosing the right profile picture is a crucial aspect of creating a strong presence on LinkedIn. Your profile picture is the first impression you make on potential connections and employers, so it's important to choose a picture that presents you in a professional and approachable manner.

Here are some key considerations and tips for selecting the perfect profile picture:

- **Professionalism**: LinkedIn is a professional networking platform, so your profile picture should reflect that. Opt for a photo that conveys a professional image and aligns with your industry and desired professional image. Dress appropriately for your field, whether that means formal attire or business casual.

- **Clear and High-Quality**: Ensure that your profile picture is clear and high-resolution. Blurry or pixelated images can create a negative impression. A well-lit and focused photo will help you appear more professional and competent.

- **Approachability**: While maintaining professionalism, it's important to appear approachable and friendly. A warm smile can go a long way in building rapport with others. Avoid overly serious or stern expressions, as they may make you seem unapproachable.

- **Focus on Your Face**: Your face should be the focal point of the picture, occupying a significant portion of the frame. This allows others to easily recognize you. Avoid using group photos or images where you are too far away, as this can make it difficult for others to identify you.

- **Neutral Background:** Choose a simple and neutral background that doesn't distract from your face. A plain wall or a professional setting can work well. Avoid busy or cluttered backgrounds that may divert attention from you.

- **Professional Headshots**: If you have the opportunity, consider getting a professional headshot taken. Professional photographers have the expertise to capture you in the best light, ensuring a polished and high-quality image.

- **Consistency**: It's advisable to use the same profile picture across your professional online presence. This helps create recognition and reinforces your personal brand. Using consistent images also ensures that connections can easily identify you when they come across your profile elsewhere.

- **Relevance**: Consider the industry and audience you are targeting on LinkedIn. If you work in a creative field, you might have more flexibility to showcase your personality through your picture. However, if you are in a more traditional or corporate industry, it's best to stick to a more conservative and professional image.

- **Avoid Distractions**: Avoid using props or accessories that may distract viewers from your face. This includes excessive jewelry, hats, sunglasses, or anything that may take away attention from your professional appearance.

Remember, your profile picture is just one element of your LinkedIn presence. Pair it with a well-crafted headline, a compelling summary, and a complete and up-to-date profile to make a strong impact on potential connections and employers.

2.3 Crafting an Attention-grabbing Headline

Crafting an attention-grabbing headline on LinkedIn is crucial to capturing the interest of potential connections and employers and increasing your visibility on the platform. A compelling headline not only grabs attention but also conveys your professional identity and expertise. In this section, I will provide you with some key tips and strategies to create a headline that stands out from the crowd and effectively showcases your professional brand.

★ **Be Clear and Specific**: Your headline should clearly convey who you are and what you do in just a few words. Avoid vague terms or buzzwords that don't provide any meaningful information (or avoid using jargon or industry-specific terms that may confuse people). Instead, Use simple and straightforward language to ensure that your headline is easily understandable to a wide range of professionals. Focus on highlighting your unique skills, expertise, or industry niche. For example, instead of simply saying "Marketing Professional," consider "Digital Marketing Strategist | SEO Specialist | Content Creator."

★ **Highlight Key Achievements**: Including notable achievements or accolades in your headline can instantly capture attention and demonstrate your value. If you've received awards, certifications, or have notable accomplishments, incorporate them into your headline. For instance, "Award-Winning Graphic Designer | Certified Adobe Expert."

★ **Use Keywords**: Incorporating relevant keywords in your headline can enhance your visibility in LinkedIn searches. Research and identify industry-specific keywords that recruiters or potential connections are likely to search for or might use or when searching for professionals in your field, and include them naturally in your headline. This will help you appear in searches related to your area of expertise. For example, if you're a software engineer specializing in machine learning, include keywords like "AI," "Python," or "Data Science" in your headline.

★ **Show Your Unique Selling Proposition**: What sets you apart from others in your industry? Highlight your unique selling proposition in your headline to pique curiosity and differentiate yourself. Whether it's your diverse background, specific expertise, or a unique perspective, communicate it concisely. For instance, "Multilingual Finance Professional | Cross-Cultural Expertise."

★ **Quantify Results**: Whenever possible, quantify your achievements to demonstrate tangible results. Numbers tend to catch attention and lend credibility to your headline. For example, instead of saying "Experienced Project Manager," try "Project Manager | Delivered $5M in Cost Savings | Led Cross-Functional Teams."

★ Adding specific details and quantifiable achievements to your headline can make it more compelling. Instead of using generic statements, include measurable results or specific projects you have worked on. This not only demonstrates your expertise but also helps potential employers or clients understand the value you can bring to their organization.

★ **Be Authentic**: While it's essential to be professional, don't be afraid to infuse your personality into your headline. This can help you stand out and create a memorable impression. Consider incorporating a touch of creativity or humor, but make sure it aligns with your personal brand and industry norms.

★ **Show your passion and personality**: Let your personality shine through your headline. LinkedIn is a professional platform, but that doesn't mean you have to be boring. Infuse your headline with enthusiasm and passion for what you do. A unique and genuine headline can make you more memorable and differentiate you from others in your field.

★ **Customize for your target audience**: Tailor your headline to resonate with your target audience. Consider the specific industry, job function, or demographic you are trying to attract, and craft a headline that speaks directly to them. Use language and keywords that are relevant to their interests and needs.

★ **Keep it Concise**: LinkedIn headlines have a character limit, so aim to keep your headline concise and to the point. A shorter headline is more likely to be read and understood quickly. Aim for a length of around 120 characters or less to ensure it's visible on both desktop and mobile devices.

★ **Test and Update:** Your headline isn't set in stone. As you progress in your career or if you're targeting different opportunities, don't hesitate to update and refine your headline accordingly. Regularly test different variations to see which ones generate more engagement or resonate better with your target audience.

★ Test and iteration are including professional networking, job search capabilities, personal branding opportunities, learning resources, business development possibilities, reputation management tools, access to industry insights, and mentorship opportunities. s very important. Don't be afraid to experiment with different headlines to see which ones perform best.

LinkedIn allows you to change your headline easily, so take advantage of this flexibility.

Monitor the response you receive from different headlines and adjust accordingly based on the feedback and engagement you receive.

Remember, your headline is a powerful tool because it is one of the first things people see when they visit your LinkedIn profile. By following these tips and customizing your headline to reflect your unique professional identity, you can maximize your chances of grabbing attention and standing out from the crowd. It can also make a strong first impression, attract the right audience, and increase your professional opportunities on LinkedIn.

2.4 Writing a Compelling Summary

A compelling summary is a crucial component of your LinkedIn profile as it serves as your professional introduction and an opportunity to grab the attention of potential connections, employers, and clients. Your summary serves as an elevator pitch. It should effectively showcase your unique value proposition, highlight your expertise, and convey your professional brand.

Here are some key tips for writing a compelling summary on your LinkedIn profile:

★ **Start with a captivating opening**: Begin your summary with a strong opening sentence or two that immediately captures the reader's interest. It could be a thought-provoking question, a powerful statement, or a brief overview of your professional journey.

Remember, your summary should be a captivating statement or a brief description of your expertise and passion. This should immediately grab the reader's attention and encourage them to keep reading.

★ **Define your professional identity**: Clearly state your professional identity and the role you aspire to or currently hold. Use concise and impactful language to describe yourself and the value you bring to the table.

★ **Highlight your unique strengths**: Identify and emphasize your unique skills, experiences, and accomplishments that set you apart from others in your field. Focus on your core competencies and the specific expertise that makes you valuable to potential employers or clients.

★ **Showcase your achievements**: Share notable achievements and success stories that demonstrate your capabilities and the impact you have made in your previous roles. Use quantifiable metrics whenever possible to provide concrete evidence of your accomplishments.

★ **Showcase your unique value proposition**: Clearly communicate what sets you apart from others in your industry. What unique skills, knowledge, or experiences do you bring to the table? Highlight how you have added value to previous roles or projects and how you can contribute to future endeavors.

★ **Tailor it to your target audience**: Consider your target audience when crafting your summary. Think about who you want to attract and tailor your messaging accordingly. Highlight the skills, experiences, and qualifications that are most relevant and appealing to your desired connections or employers.

★ **Share your professional goals**: Briefly outline your career aspirations and the type of opportunities you are seeking. This helps others understand your motivations and align their interests with yours. However, avoid being too specific or limiting your options too much.

★ **Personalize your summary**: While maintaining a professional tone, don't be afraid to inject your personality into your summary by sharing your passions, interests, or personal values. This humanizes your profile and allows others to connect with you on a more personal level. It also lets your authentic voice shine through and give readers a glimpse into your professional persona which can help you establish a personal connection and stand out from the crowd.

★ **Incorporate keywords**: Incorporate relevant keywords throughout your summary to optimize your profile's visibility in LinkedIn searches and increase your chances of being discovered by recruiters or potential clients. Think about the terms and phrases that potential employers or clients might use when looking for someone with your expertise and include them strategically. This will enhance your visibility and attract the right opportunities.

★ **Keep it concise and scannable**: LinkedIn summaries should be concise and easily scannable. Use short paragraphs (aim for a length of around 3-5 concise paragraphs), bullet points (or a maximum of 2-3 bulleted sections), and subheadings or bold text to break up the text and make it easier for readers to skim through. Focus on the most important information and avoid unnecessary details.

* **Include a call to action**: Conclude your summary with a call to action, such as inviting others to connect, reach out for collaboration, or visit your website or portfolio. This encourages engagement and further interaction with your profile.

* **Proofread and revise**: Before publishing your summary, carefully proofread it for any grammatical or spelling errors. Review and revise the content to ensure it flows smoothly and effectively communicates your message.

* **Regularly update and refine**: Your LinkedIn profile should be a living document that evolves with your professional journey. Regularly review and update your summary to reflect your latest accomplishments, skills, and goals. Continuously refine it to ensure it remains compelling and aligned with your professional brand.

Remember, a compelling summary on LinkedIn can make a significant impact on your profile's effectiveness as It's an opportunity to showcase your unique professional brand and make a memorable impression. By crafting a concise, engaging, and personalized summary that highlights your unique value proposition, you increase your chances of attracting the right connections, opportunities, and career advancements.

2.5 Showcasing your Experience and Skills

Showcasing your experience and skills effectively on LinkedIn is crucial for building a strong professional profile and attracting opportunities.

In this section, I'll provide you with comprehensive tips on how to highlight your experience and skills to maximize your LinkedIn presence.

★ Craft a Compelling Headline:

Your LinkedIn headline is the first thing people see, so make it impactful. Instead of simply listing your job title, consider adding a value proposition or key skills to grab attention. For example, "Digital Marketing Strategist | SEO Specialist | Helping Businesses Drive Online Success."

★ Write a Captivating Summary:

Utilize the summary section to provide a concise overview of your background, expertise, and career goals. Focus on highlighting your unique value proposition, key accomplishments, and the impact you've made in previous roles. Use keywords relevant to your industry to optimize your profile for search results.

★ **Optimize Your Experience Section:**

When listing your experience, go beyond job titles and include detailed descriptions of your responsibilities, achievements, and notable projects. Be results-oriented and quantify your accomplishments whenever possible. This helps potential employers or clients understand your capabilities and the value you can bring to their organization.

★ **Showcase Projects and Work Samples:**

LinkedIn allows you to showcase your work by including media attachments, such as presentations, videos, or articles. Leverage this feature to display your portfolio, case studies, or any relevant samples that demonstrate your skills and expertise. This visually enhances your profile and provides tangible evidence of your capabilities.

★ **Request Recommendations:**

Ask colleagues, managers, and clients for recommendations on LinkedIn. These testimonials validate your skills and experience, boosting your credibility. Aim for well-rounded recommendations that highlight different aspects of your work, such as leadership, collaboration, or technical expertise.

★ Highlight Skills and Endorsements:

Include a comprehensive list of relevant skills on your profile. LinkedIn offers a specific section for this purpose. Be strategic in selecting skills that align with your target roles or industry. Additionally, actively seek endorsements from your connections to validate your proficiency in these skills.

★ Engage in Thought Leadership:

Position yourself as an industry expert by sharing valuable content, insights, and opinions on LinkedIn. Publish articles, contribute to discussions, or share relevant news and resources. This demonstrates your knowledge, passion, and commitment to staying up-to-date in your field.

★ Join Relevant Groups and Communities:

Participate in LinkedIn groups and communities related to your industry or areas of expertise. Engage in discussions, offer insights, and connect with like-minded professionals. This not only expands your network but also exposes you to new opportunities and keeps you informed about industry trends.

★ Actively Network and Connect:

Build and nurture your professional network by actively connecting with colleagues, industry peers, and potential employers. Personalize connection requests and engage in meaningful conversations. Be proactive in seeking out new connections, attending industry events, and leveraging LinkedIn's advanced search features to find professionals who align with your career goals.

★ Regularly Update and Maintain Your Profile:

Lastly, ensure that your LinkedIn profile is up to date and reflects your current skills, experiences, and achievements. Regularly review and refresh your profile to align with your career progression. Engage with your network by sharing updates and staying connected with relevant industry trends.

By following these tips, you'll be able to effectively showcase your experience and skills on LinkedIn, attracting the attention of potential employers, clients, and professional opportunities. Remember to stay engaged, consistent, and authentic in your LinkedIn interactions to maximize the benefits of its powerful professional platform.

2.6 Adding Education and Certifications

Adding education and certifications to your LinkedIn profile is crucial for showcasing your professional qualifications, enhancing your credibility, and increasing your chances of attracting relevant opportunities. These sections provide valuable information to potential employers, clients, or collaborators and allow you to highlight your expertise and commitment to continuous learning. In this section, we will explore the best practices for adding education and certifications to your LinkedIn profile.

★ Education Section:

The education section on LinkedIn allows you to list your academic background, including degrees, diplomas, and courses you have completed. Follow these tips to make the most of this section:

a. **Start with your highest level of education**: Begin by entering your most recent degree or the one most relevant to your career goals. Include the degree title, field of study, and the institution where you received it. If you graduated with honors, mention that as well.

b. **Provide additional degrees and certifications**: If you have multiple degrees or certifications, list them in chronological order, starting with the most recent one. Include the degree or certification name, the institution or certifying body, and the completion date.

c. **Add relevant coursework or projects**: If you undertook coursework or projects that are relevant to your career or demonstrate specific skills, mention them in bullet points. This can help you stand out and show practical application of your education.

d. **Include academic achievements or awards**: If you received any honors, awards, or scholarships during your academic journey, highlight them. This information can further enhance your profile and demonstrate your dedication and exceptional performance.

★ **Certifications Section:**

LinkedIn's certifications section is specifically designed for showcasing professional certifications, licenses, and training programs you have completed. Follow these guidelines when adding certifications:

a. **Include industry-relevant certifications**: List certifications that are relevant to your field or industry. This could include professional certifications, specialized training programs, or licenses that showcase your expertise.

b. **Include certification details**: Specify the name of the certification, the issuing organization or authority, and the completion date. If applicable, mention any notable achievements associated with the certification, such as earning a high score or receiving a specialized designation.

c. **Add descriptions or bullet points**: Utilize the 2,000-character description field to provide additional information about the certification. You can mention key topics covered, skills gained, or any notable projects associated with the certification.

d. **Showcase your active certifications**: If you have certifications that require regular renewal or ongoing professional development, make sure to update them as soon as you complete any necessary requirements or obtain a new version of the certification.

★ **Additional Tips:**

a. **Order your education and certifications strategically**: Place your education and certifications sections after your professional experience to ensure that recruiters and visitors see your relevant work history first. This helps to highlight your practical experience and expertise before delving into your educational background.

b. Provide context through descriptions: In both the education and certifications sections, consider adding brief descriptions or bullet points that elaborate on the skills, knowledge, or accomplishments associated with your qualifications. This can provide additional context and help potential connections understand the value you bring.

c. Utilize multimedia and documents: LinkedIn allows you to upload supporting documents, such as transcripts, course completion certificates, or project portfolios. If applicable, include these to provide further evidence of your educational achievements or certifications.

d. Regularly update your profile: Keep your education and certifications sections up to date with any new degrees, certifications, or completed courses. This shows your commitment to professional growth and keeps your profile relevant.

Overall, adding education and certifications to your LinkedIn profile is essential for establishing your professional credibility and expertise. By following these best practices and regularly updating your profile, you can effectively showcase your qualifications and increase your chances of attracting valuable career opportunities. Remember, a well-documented educational background and a comprehensive list of certifications can greatly enhance your LinkedIn profile's overall impact and strengthen your professional brand.

2.7 Optimizing your profile for search

This is basically a recap of the steps involved in setting up your LinkedIn profile.

LinkedIn is a powerful platform for professional networking and job searching. With millions of users and numerous companies actively recruiting, it is essential to optimize your profile to stand out in search results. By implementing effective optimization strategies, you can increase your visibility and improve your chances of being discovered by potential employers, clients, or professional connections. In this section, we will explore key steps to optimize your LinkedIn profile for enhanced search visibility.

★ Selecting the Right Keywords:

Keywords play a crucial role in optimizing your LinkedIn profile for search. Identify relevant keywords that reflect your industry, skills, job titles, and areas of expertise. Conduct thorough research to understand the specific terms and phrases commonly used in your field. Incorporate these keywords naturally throughout your profile, including your headline, summary, experience descriptions, and skill section. By aligning your profile with targeted keywords, you increase the likelihood of appearing in search results when recruiters or professionals search for those terms.

★ Craft a Compelling Headline:

Your headline is one of the first elements people see when they come across your profile. Instead of simply stating your current job title, use this space to highlight your unique value proposition and key skills. Be concise, creative, and specific, as this will capture attention and encourage professionals to click on your profile.

★ Write a Strong Summary:

Your LinkedIn summary provides an opportunity to showcase your professional story and accomplishments. Optimize it by incorporating relevant keywords and emphasizing your expertise and experience. Craft a compelling narrative that captures your strengths, highlights your achievements, and conveys your career aspirations. Engage your audience by sharing your unique perspective and demonstrating your value proposition.

★ Optimize Experience Descriptions:

When detailing your professional experience, optimize your descriptions by providing clear and concise summaries of your roles and responsibilities. Highlight key achievements, quantifiable results, and the impact you made in each position. Utilize relevant keywords throughout the descriptions to improve search visibility and ensure that your accomplishments align with the expectations of your target audience.

★ Highlight Skills and Endorsements:

LinkedIn's skills section enables you to showcase your competencies and strengths. Include a diverse range of relevant skills and prioritize them based on their importance to your professional profile. Encourage connections to endorse your skills, as endorsements add credibility to your profile and improve your search ranking for those particular skills.

★ Network and Engage:

Engagement is essential on LinkedIn. Actively participate in relevant industry groups, share insightful content, and interact with other professionals in your network. Regularly comment on and share articles, posts, and updates related to your industry. By demonstrating your expertise and engaging with others, you enhance your visibility and increase the likelihood of being discovered by potential employers or connections.

★ Obtain Recommendations:

LinkedIn recommendations serve as powerful testimonials from colleagues, clients, or supervisors. Request recommendations from individuals who can vouch for your skills, work ethic, and achievements. These recommendations not only enhance your profile's credibility but also improve its search visibility.

★ Customize Your Public Profile URL:

LinkedIn allows you to customize your public profile URL, making it easier to share and optimize for search engines. Include your name or relevant keywords in the URL to enhance your visibility in search results outside of LinkedIn.

Overall, optimizing your LinkedIn profile for enhanced search visibility is vital for career growth and professional opportunities. By selecting appropriate keywords, crafting a compelling headline and summary, optimizing experience descriptions, highlighting skills, actively engaging with your network, obtaining recommendations, and customizing your public profile URL, you significantly increase your chances of being discovered by the right audience. Implement these strategies, and make your LinkedIn profile stand out from the crowd, ultimately opening doors to new career prospects, networking opportunities, and professional success.

Chapter 3: Building Your Professional Network

3.1 Connecting with Colleagues and Classmates

Connecting with colleagues and classmates on LinkedIn is a valuable practice that can significantly enhance your professional network and open doors to new opportunities. Leveraging this platform effectively allows you to maintain meaningful relationships, stay updated on industry developments, and collaborate with like-minded individuals. In this section, I will provide insights and strategies to help you connect with colleagues and classmates on LinkedIn in a meaningful and professional manner.

★ **Optimize your LinkedIn profile**: Before connecting with colleagues and classmates, ensure that your LinkedIn profile is complete and showcases your professional achievements, skills, and experiences. Use a professional profile picture, craft a compelling headline, and write a concise summary that highlights your expertise. Remember to include relevant keywords to make your profile more discoverable.

★ **Personalize connection requests:** When sending connection requests, avoid using the default message. Instead, take a moment to personalize your message by mentioning a shared experience, such as a project you worked on together or a class you attended. This personal touch demonstrates your genuine interest in reconnecting and increases the likelihood of your request being accepted.

★ **Utilize LinkedIn Alumni and Classmates features**: LinkedIn offers specific features like "Alumni" and "Classmates" that enable you to search for and connect with people who attended the same educational institution or were part of the same graduating class. These features make it easier to find and reconnect with former classmates, fostering a sense of community and allowing you to tap into shared experiences and resources.

★ **Engage with shared content**: Actively engage with content shared by your colleagues and classmates on LinkedIn. Like, comment, and share their posts to demonstrate your support and interest in their professional endeavors. Engaging with their content not only strengthens your existing relationships but also expands your visibility within their networks.

★ **Join relevant LinkedIn groups**: Seek out and join LinkedIn groups related to your industry, alma mater, or specific areas of interest.

Engaging in group discussions and sharing valuable insights positions you as a knowledgeable professional and provides opportunities to connect with like-minded individuals, including both colleagues and classmates.

★ **Attend and organize virtual events**: LinkedIn offers a wide range of virtual events, such as webinars, workshops, and industry conferences. Participating in these events allows you to connect with professionals from various backgrounds, including your colleagues and classmates. Take advantage of the networking features within these events to initiate conversations and strengthen your connections.

★ **Offer and seek recommendations**: Recommendations play a crucial role in establishing credibility and trust on LinkedIn. Offer recommendations to your colleagues and classmates for their outstanding work or skills, and kindly request recommendations from those you have collaborated with. These recommendations act as endorsements, enhancing your professional reputation and increasing your chances of connecting with others.

★ **Stay in touch**: Connecting with colleagues and classmates on LinkedIn is just the beginning. To build and maintain strong relationships, make an effort to stay in touch beyond the platform. Consider scheduling coffee chats, video calls, or attending industry events together. Nurturing these relationships strengthens your network and creates a support system for your professional journey.

Remember, when connecting with colleagues and classmates on LinkedIn, it's essential to approach each interaction with professionalism and respect. Build relationships based on mutual value and shared interests, and always strive to provide support and assistance to others in your network. By leveraging the power of LinkedIn, you can strengthen your professional connections, expand your knowledge base, and unlock new opportunities throughout your career.

3.2 Reaching out to Industry Professionals

Reaching out to industry professionals on LinkedIn is a valuable strategy for networking, building connections, and expanding your professional opportunities. When done effectively, it can lead to collaborations, job opportunities, mentorship, and access to valuable industry insights.

Here are some key tips to help you successfully connect with industry professionals on LinkedIn:

★ **Define your objective**: Before reaching out to professionals, clearly define your goal or purpose. Are you seeking career advice, job opportunities, partnership opportunities, or simply expanding your network? Having a clear objective will help you tailor your outreach messages and make your intentions clear to the professionals you're reaching out to.

★ **Personalize your message**: When initiating contact, it's essential to personalize your message for each professional you're reaching out to. Avoid generic templates or copy-pasting the same message to multiple individuals. Start by addressing the person by name and briefly mention why you're interested in connecting with them specifically.

Highlight any common interests, achievements, or connections you may share. Personalization demonstrates genuine interest and increases the likelihood of a positive response.

★ **Be concise and respectful**: Industry professionals are often busy, so it's important to be concise and respectful of their time. Keep your initial message brief, focusing on the most relevant points. Introduce yourself briefly, explain your reason for reaching out, and express your admiration for their work or achievements. Avoid lengthy explanations or irrelevant information that may distract from your main purpose.

★ **Demonstrate value**: To make your outreach message compelling, it's important to communicate the value you can offer to the professional you're contacting. Highlight any skills, experiences, or insights that are relevant to their field or interests. Share specific examples of how you can contribute to their work or industry. Offering value upfront increases the chances of a positive response and encourages professionals to engage with you.

* **Engage with their content**: Before reaching out, take the time to research the professional's LinkedIn profile, posts, and articles. Engage with their content by liking, commenting, or sharing their posts. This demonstrates genuine interest and familiarity with their work. When reaching out, mention a specific piece of content they shared that resonated with you and explain why. It helps to establish a connection and shows that you've done your homework.

* **Maintain a professional tone**: While LinkedIn is a professional networking platform, it's important to strike the right tone in your outreach messages. Keep your language polite, professional, and friendly. Avoid using overly informal or casual language that may be perceived as unprofessional. Present yourself as a serious and respectful individual who values their time and expertise.

* **Follow up appropriately**: If you don't receive a response immediately, don't be discouraged. Industry professionals are often inundated with messages and may take time to respond. Wait for a reasonable period (around 1-2 weeks) before sending a polite follow-up message. In the follow-up, reiterate your interest and politely ask if they had a chance to consider your previous message. Avoid being pushy or demanding and respect their decision if they choose not to respond.

Remember, networking is a two-way street. Offer support, knowledge, or assistance when appropriate, and be open to reciprocating favors or information in return. Building meaningful connections takes time and effort, so be patient and persistent in your outreach efforts. With a thoughtful and personalized approach, LinkedIn can be a powerful platform for connecting with industry professionals and advancing your career.

3.3 Engaging with LinkedIn Groups

Engaging with LinkedIn Groups can be a highly effective strategy for professionals looking to expand their network, establish thought leadership, and create meaningful connections within their industry. LinkedIn Groups provide a platform for like-minded individuals to gather, share insights, and engage in discussions relevant to their professional interests. In this section, we will explore key tips and strategies to help you maximize your engagement within LinkedIn Groups.

★ **Find and Join Relevant Groups**: Start by identifying LinkedIn Groups that align with your professional goals and interests. Look for groups that have an active and engaged community, as well as a focus on topics that are relevant to your industry or area of expertise.

You can use LinkedIn's search function to discover groups or browse the "Groups" tab on the LinkedIn homepage.

★ **Review Group Guidelines and Rules**: Once you've found a group of interest, carefully review the group guidelines and rules to understand the community's expectations. Familiarize yourself with the group's purpose, posting guidelines, and any restrictions that may be in place. Adhering to these guidelines will help you build a positive reputation within the group.

★ **Observe and Listen**: Before jumping into discussions, take some time to observe the group dynamics and understand the types of conversations that are taking place. Pay attention to the topics being discussed, the level of engagement, and the influential members within the group. This observation will give you insights into the group's culture and help you tailor your contributions accordingly.

★ **Provide Value**: When engaging in LinkedIn Groups, focus on adding value to the discussions. Share your expertise, insights, and relevant experiences that can contribute to the conversation. Avoid self-promotion or overly salesy messages, as these may be seen as spam and can harm your professional reputation.

Instead, aim to be helpful, informative, and authentic in your interactions.

★ **Ask Thoughtful Questions**: Asking well-thought-out questions is an excellent way to initiate discussions and encourage others to participate. Craft questions that spark meaningful conversations and invite different perspectives. This can help you establish yourself as a thought leader and attract attention from other group members.

★ **Respond and Engage**: Actively participate in ongoing discussions by responding to comments, sharing your opinions, and engaging with other members' posts. Be respectful and considerate in your interactions, even when there are differing opinions. Constructive debates and exchanges can lead to valuable insights and expand your professional network.

★ **Share Relevant Content**: LinkedIn Groups provide an opportunity to share valuable content with a targeted audience. If you come across articles, blog posts, or resources that are relevant to the group's interests, share them with a brief introduction or commentary to encourage discussion. However, be cautious not to excessively promote your own content.

★ **Network and Connect**: LinkedIn Groups offer a unique opportunity to network with professionals in your industry or area of interest. Engage with individuals whose contributions resonate with you and establish connections by sending personalized connection requests. Personalize your messages to express your interest in their work or contributions within the group.

★ **Be Consistent and Regular**: Building relationships and establishing credibility within LinkedIn Groups takes time and consistency. Regularly engage with the group by contributing to discussions, offering insights, and sharing valuable content. By being consistently present and active, you can nurture relationships and make a lasting impact within the group.

★ **Monitor Notifications and Manage Time**: LinkedIn Groups can generate a significant amount of activity and notifications. It's important to manage your time effectively and avoid getting overwhelmed. Set aside dedicated time to engage with the groups you've joined, and adjust your notification settings to receive updates that are most relevant to you.

Remember, the key to successful engagement in LinkedIn Groups is to be genuine, provide value, and foster meaningful connections.

By following these tips and strategies, you can leverage the power of LinkedIn Groups to expand your professional network, enhance your reputation, and stay up-to-date with industry trends and insights. Engaging with LinkedIn Groups is an ongoing process that requires dedication and consistent effort, but the rewards can be significant.

3.4 Expanding your network strategically

Expanding your network strategically on LinkedIn is essential for professional growth and success. Building a strong and diverse network opens up new opportunities, enhances your visibility, and allows you to tap into valuable resources.

Here are some key strategies to help you expand your network effectively:

* ★ **Define your networking goals:** Before you start connecting with others, clarify your objectives. Identify the specific industries, roles, or individuals you want to connect with to align with your professional aspirations. Having a clear focus will help you build a targeted network.

★ **Optimize your LinkedIn profile**: Your LinkedIn profile serves as your professional online presence. Ensure that your profile is complete, up-to-date, and compelling. Use a professional photo, write a concise and engaging headline, and provide a compelling summary that showcases your expertise and value proposition.

★ **Leverage existing connections**: Start by reaching out to your existing contacts, such as colleagues, classmates, and industry peers. Utilize LinkedIn's "People You May Know" feature to discover potential connections based on mutual connections or shared interests.

★ **Join relevant groups and communities**: Participating in LinkedIn groups and communities that align with your professional interests and goals is an effective way to expand your network. Engage in meaningful discussions, share valuable insights, and connect with like-minded professionals.

★ **Engage with content**: Regularly engage with relevant content by liking, commenting, and sharing posts that resonate with you. This not only helps you stay visible but also fosters connections with individuals who share similar interests or perspectives.

★ **Personalize connection requests**: When sending connection requests, take the time to personalize your messages. Mention common interests, shared connections, or specific reasons why you'd like to connect. A personalized approach increases the likelihood of your request being accepted.

★ **Attend events and webinars**: LinkedIn offers various events and webinars, both virtual and in-person, that provide valuable networking opportunities. Participate in these events to connect with professionals in your industry, ask insightful questions, and share your expertise.

★ **Be proactive and reach out**: Don't be afraid to initiate conversations with individuals you admire or professionals in positions you aspire to. Send thoughtful messages expressing your interest in their work or seeking advice. Building genuine relationships is a key aspect of strategic networking.

★ **Offer value to others**: Networking is a two-way street. Look for opportunities to provide value to your connections. Share relevant articles or resources, offer assistance or guidance, and actively support and promote the work of others. By being helpful, you can strengthen your relationships and expand your network.

★ **Maintain and nurture your network**: Building a network is not a one-time activity; it requires consistent effort. Regularly engage with your connections by congratulating them on their achievements, commenting on their posts, and reaching out periodically to stay connected. Building and maintaining relationships is key to unlocking opportunities.

Remember, networking is about building mutually beneficial relationships. Approach it with authenticity, professionalism, and a genuine interest in others. By strategically expanding your network on LinkedIn, you can amplify your professional presence, gain insights from industry leaders, and unlock new opportunities for career growth.

3.5 Building relationships through personalized messages

Building relationships through personalized messages is a crucial aspect of effective networking on LinkedIn. In a digital age where interactions are often impersonal and transactional, taking the time to craft personalized messages can make a significant difference in creating meaningful connections. Here are some key tips for building relationships through personalized messages on LinkedIn:

★ **Research and Personalization**: Before reaching out to someone, take the time to research their profile, interests, and professional background. Look for commonalities such as shared experiences, mutual connections, or shared interests.

Use this information to personalize your message and demonstrate that you have taken the time to understand them.

★ **Start with a Warm Greeting**: Begin your message with a warm and professional greeting, addressing the person by their name. Avoid generic and impersonal openings, as they can come across as automated and insincere. Starting on a friendly note helps create a positive impression from the start.

★ **Highlight Common Ground**: When crafting your message, focus on highlighting any common ground or shared interests you discovered during your research. This could include attending the same university, working in similar industries, or participating in the same professional groups. Mentioning these commonalities can help establish a rapport and make your message more relatable.

★ **Be Specific and Purposeful**: Clearly state the purpose of your message and be specific about why you are reaching out. Whether it's requesting advice, seeking a collaboration, or expressing admiration for their work, ensure your intentions are clear. Being purposeful demonstrates that you value their time and are genuinely interested in building a relationship.

★ **Personalize the Content:** Tailor the content of your message to the individual you are contacting. Avoid generic templates or copy-pasted messages. Instead, include specific details that show you have invested effort into understanding their background and achievements. This personal touch demonstrates authenticity and helps your message stand out.

★ **Offer Value**: When reaching out to someone on LinkedIn, consider how you can provide value to them. This could involve sharing relevant articles, offering insights or resources, or suggesting ways you can collaborate. Offering something of value demonstrates your willingness to contribute and fosters reciprocity, enhancing the chances of building a strong relationship.

★ **Respect Boundaries and Timing**: LinkedIn is a professional platform, and it's essential to respect boundaries and be mindful of timing. Avoid being overly persistent or pushy if someone doesn't respond immediately. Give them time to review and respond to your message at their own pace. Remember, building relationships takes time and patience.

★ **Follow Up Appropriately**: If you don't receive a response to your initial message, don't be discouraged.

It's common for professionals to be busy and miss or overlook messages. A polite and considerate follow-up message can be appropriate after a reasonable interval. However, avoid being too persistent or demanding.

★ **Maintain Professionalism**: Throughout your communication, maintain a professional tone and language. Avoid using slang or overly informal expressions, unless it aligns with the recipient's style of communication. Keep your messages concise, respectful, and free of typos or grammatical errors.

★ **Nurture the Relationship:** Building relationships doesn't end with the initial message. Invest time in nurturing the connection by engaging with the person's content, commenting on their posts, or sharing relevant information. Building a genuine relationship requires ongoing effort and mutual engagement.

Remember, personalized messages are essential for building strong and lasting relationships on LinkedIn. By demonstrating genuine interest, offering value, and maintaining professionalism, you can create meaningful connections that can lead to fruitful collaborations, mentorships, or career opportunities.

Chapter 4: Leveraging LinkedIn's Features

4.1 Job search and career opportunities

In this section, we will explore key tips and best practices to enhance your job search and discover exciting career opportunities.

1. Building a Strong LinkedIn Profile:

LinkedIn has become an essential tool for job seekers. To increase your chances of finding relevant career opportunities, it is crucial to create a compelling and professional LinkedIn profile. Here are some key elements to focus on:

- Profile Picture: Choose a high-quality, friendly, and professional headshot to make a positive first impression.
- Headline: Craft a concise headline that highlights your expertise, skills, and career aspirations.
- Summary: Write a compelling summary that showcases your accomplishments, experiences, and unique value proposition.
- Experience: Include detailed information about your work experience, highlighting key achievements and responsibilities.
- Skills and Endorsements: Add relevant skills and seek endorsements from colleagues, supervisors, or clients.
- Recommendations: Request recommendations from former colleagues or supervisors to strengthen your profile's credibility.

2. Utilizing LinkedIn Job Search Features:

LinkedIn offers a range of features and tools to aid your job search. Here are some tips to make the most of them:

- Job Search Filters: Use advanced search filters to refine your job search based on location, industry, experience level, and more.
- Saved Searches: Set up saved searches to receive email notifications about new job postings that match your criteria.
- Job Alerts: Activate job alerts to receive instant notifications when new positions become available.
- Apply Directly on LinkedIn: Many employers allow candidates to apply directly through LinkedIn. Take advantage of this feature to streamline your application process.

3. Networking and Connections:

Networking is a crucial aspect of job searching. Leverage LinkedIn's extensive professional network to expand your connections and increase your visibility to potential employers. Here are some networking tips:

- Connect with Industry Professionals: Send personalized connection requests to professionals in your desired industry, including recruiters, hiring managers, and colleagues.

- Join LinkedIn Groups: Participate in relevant LinkedIn groups and engage in discussions to showcase your expertise and expand your network.
- Attend Virtual Events: LinkedIn frequently hosts virtual events and webinars focused on professional development and networking. Participate in these events to connect with industry leaders and fellow job seekers.

4. Engaging with Company Pages:

LinkedIn offers company pages where organizations post job openings and share updates. Here's how you can leverage them:

- Follow Target Companies: Identify companies of interest and follow their LinkedIn pages to stay updated on their latest news, job postings, and company culture.
- Engage with Content: Like, comment, and share relevant content from company pages to demonstrate your interest and engage with potential employers.
- Research Company Insights: Explore a company's LinkedIn page to gain valuable insights about their values, culture, and current employees.

5. Leveraging Recommendations and Endorsements:

Strong recommendations and endorsements can significantly enhance your job search. Here's how to leverage them:

- Request Recommendations: Reach out to former colleagues, supervisors, or clients and request recommendations that highlight your skills, work ethic, and accomplishments.
- Provide Recommendations: Offer to write recommendations for your connections. This gesture can often prompt them to reciprocate and provide recommendations for you as well.
- Seek Endorsements: Actively seek endorsements for your skills from your network. These endorsements add credibility and validate your expertise.

6. Upgrading Skills and Professional Development:

To stand out in a competitive job market, continuous learning and professional development are essential. Here are some ways to upgrade your skills:

- LinkedIn Learning: Take advantage of LinkedIn Learning, a platform offering a vast array of online courses covering various topics and skills. Enhance your skills and knowledge in areas relevant to your desired career path.

- Certifications: Identify industry-specific certifications that can boost your qualifications and make you more attractive to potential employers.
- Professional Associations: Join professional associations related to your field and participate in workshops, conferences, and networking events to stay updated on industry trends and expand your knowledge.

7. Customizing Applications and Tailoring Resumes:

Each job opportunity is unique, and it's crucial to customize your application materials accordingly. Consider the following tips:

- Tailor Your Resume: Customize your resume for each job application, highlighting relevant skills, experiences, and achievements that align with the requirements of the position.
- Cover Letters: Craft a compelling cover letter that showcases your enthusiasm for the role, addresses specific job requirements, and explains how your skills and experiences make you a strong fit.
- Research the Company: Thoroughly research the company before applying. Familiarize yourself with their values, mission, and culture to align your application with their needs.

8. Maintaining an Active Presence:

Consistency is key on LinkedIn. Stay active and engaged to maximize your visibility and opportunities:

- Share Relevant Content: Regularly share industry-related articles, insights, or thought leadership pieces to demonstrate your expertise and engage with your network.
- Engage with Others: Like, comment, and share posts from your connections to foster meaningful interactions and expand your network.
- Publish LinkedIn Articles: Utilize LinkedIn's publishing platform to showcase your knowledge and perspectives on industry-related topics.

Overall, by implementing these strategies and utilizing the features and tools offered by LinkedIn, you can enhance your job search and discover exciting career opportunities. Remember to continuously upgrade your skills, engage with industry professionals, and tailor your application materials to stand out in the competitive job market. LinkedIn serves as a powerful platform to connect with employers, showcase your expertise, and advance your career.

****Best of luck in your job search and career endeavors! ****

4.2 Using LinkedIn Learning for professional development

LinkedIn Learning is a valuable platform for professional development, offering a wide range of courses and resources to enhance your skills and advance your career.

Here are some key points to consider when using LinkedIn Learning for professional development:

★ **Diverse Course Catalog**: LinkedIn Learning boasts an extensive library of courses covering various subjects, including business, technology, creative skills, and more. The diverse range of courses allows professionals from different fields to find relevant content that aligns with their career goals.

★ **High-Quality Content**: The courses available on LinkedIn Learning are created and delivered by industry experts and professionals with real-world experience. This ensures that the content is of high quality and up-to-date, providing valuable insights and practical knowledge.

★ **Flexibility and Convenience**: LinkedIn Learning offers a flexible learning experience, allowing you to access courses at your own pace and convenience. The platform is available 24/7, enabling you to learn whenever and wherever you want, whether it's during your lunch break or on your daily commute.

★ **Skill Development**: LinkedIn Learning focuses on skill development, providing you with the opportunity to learn new skills or enhance existing ones. This is particularly beneficial in today's rapidly evolving job market, where staying ahead with relevant skills is crucial for professional success.

★ **Personalized Learning Paths**: The platform offers personalized learning paths based on your interests, goals, and skills. By answering a few questions about your career aspirations, LinkedIn Learning suggests relevant courses and creates a customized learning journey tailored to your needs.

★ **Certifications and Badges**: LinkedIn Learning provides the option to earn certifications and badges upon completing certain courses or learning paths. These credentials can be added to your LinkedIn profile, showcasing your commitment to professional development and increasing your visibility to potential employers.

★ **Social Learning and Collaboration**: LinkedIn Learning incorporates social learning features, allowing you to engage with peers, industry experts, and instructors. You can join relevant groups, participate in discussions, and exchange insights, fostering a collaborative learning environment.

★ **Integration with LinkedIn**: LinkedIn Learning seamlessly integrates with the LinkedIn professional networking platform. This integration enables you to showcase your completed courses and certifications on your LinkedIn profile, making it easier for potential employers to assess your skills and qualifications.

★ **Job Search Benefits**: Using LinkedIn Learning can enhance your job search efforts. By completing relevant courses and earning certifications, you can demonstrate your expertise and commitment to continuous learning, making your profile more attractive to recruiters and hiring managers.

★ **Professional Networking Opportunities**: LinkedIn Learning provides an opportunity to connect with professionals in your field of interest. Engaging in course discussions and joining relevant LinkedIn groups can expand your professional network, potentially leading to valuable connections and career opportunities.

Overall, LinkedIn Learning offers a wealth of resources and opportunities for professional development. By leveraging its diverse course catalog, high-quality content, flexibility, and integration with LinkedIn, you can acquire new skills, earn certifications, enhance your job search efforts, and expand your professional network. Make the most of this platform to advance your career and stay competitive in today's dynamic job market.

4.3 Showcasing your work with LinkedIn's portfolio feature

LinkedIn is not just a platform for networking and job searching; it also provides professionals with a range of tools to showcase their skills and accomplishments. One such feature is the portfolio feature, which allows you to display your work directly on your LinkedIn profile. By utilizing this powerful tool, you can present your projects, achievements, and expertise in a visually appealing and easily accessible manner, making a strong impression on potential employers and clients.

In this section, we will explore the benefits of utilizing LinkedIn's portfolio feature and provide you with tips on how to effectively showcase your work to enhance your professional brand and also provide practical tips on how to leverage it effectively.

i. Understanding LinkedIn's Portfolio Feature:

LinkedIn's portfolio feature allows you to visually showcase your work by attaching media files such as images, documents, presentations, videos, links and other media directly to your profile. These files can represent various types of work, including project samples, case studies, whitepapers, research papers, articles, designs, and more. This feature enables you to provide concrete evidence of your skills, projects, expertise and achievements, giving viewers a deeper understanding of your capabilities as well as helping you establish credibility and differentiate yourself in your industry.

ii. Selecting the Right Portfolio Items:

When deciding what to include in your portfolio, consider your target audience and the specific skills and experiences relevant to your industry or desired job role. Choose high-quality examples that highlight your expertise and accomplishments. Ensure that the items you showcase demonstrate your versatility, problem-solving abilities, and the value you can bring to potential employers.

iii. Creating a Structured and Engaging Portfolio:

Organize your portfolio in a structured manner to make it easy for visitors to navigate and understand your work. Consider creating separate sections or categories to showcase different types of projects or skills. Use descriptive titles and provide concise explanations or captions for each item to provide context and highlight your role or contribution.

iv. Showcasing Different Types of Work:

LinkedIn's portfolio feature supports various file formats, allowing you to exhibit a wide range of work. Consider including samples of your presentations, reports, whitepapers, design projects, code snippets, videos, or any other relevant materials. Ensure that the content is visually appealing, well-formatted, and easily digestible for viewers.

Benefits of Showcasing Your Work:

- Demonstrates your skills and expertise:

By showcasing your work through the portfolio feature, you can provide tangible examples of your abilities and demonstrate your expertise in specific areas. This visual representation adds credibility and depth to your profile, allowing potential employers or clients to assess your skills more effectively.

- Differentiates you from competitors:

A portfolio that showcases your work sets you apart from other professionals in your field. It allows you to highlight your unique accomplishments, projects, or methodologies, showcasing what makes you stand out from the crowd. This differentiation can be a significant advantage when competing for job opportunities or attracting potential clients.

- Enhances your professional brand:

LinkedIn's portfolio feature enables you to shape your professional brand by curating a collection of your best work. This collection serves as a visual representation of your professional journey, achievements, and the value you can bring to organizations or clients. It helps establish a strong and memorable professional identity that aligns with your career goals.

Tips for Effectively Showcasing Your Work:

- Leverage multimedia formats:

Utilize different media formats to present your work effectively. For example, you can include images, videos, or presentations to provide a more interactive and engaging experience. Use multimedia strategically to highlight key aspects of your work and capture viewers' attention.

- Choose relevant and high-quality examples:

Select work samples that are directly related to your industry, expertise, or the type of job you are targeting. Highlight projects that best demonstrate your skills and achievements. Ensure that the files you upload are of high quality and easily accessible by viewers.

- Provide context and descriptions:

Accompany each portfolio item with a clear and concise description that outlines the project's objectives, your role, the challenges faced, and the results achieved. This contextual information helps viewers understand the significance of your work and the value you brought to the project.

- Show diversity and breadth:

Include a variety of work samples that showcase your versatility and breadth of skills. This could include projects from different industries, collaborations with diverse teams, or examples that demonstrate your ability to tackle different types of challenges. Presenting a well-rounded portfolio reflects your adaptability and capacity to excel in various professional environments.

- Update and refresh regularly:

Keep your portfolio up to date by adding new projects, removing outdated content, and ensuring all links and files are still accessible. Regularly refreshing your portfolio demonstrates your commitment to ongoing growth and development and keeps your profile engaging and relevant.

v. Leveraging Multimedia:

While text descriptions are essential, incorporating multimedia elements can make your portfolio more engaging and memorable. Consider including videos, infographics, or interactive elements that showcase your work dynamically. Videos can be especially effective for demonstrating your skills, such as presenting a project or explaining a complex concept.

vi. Soliciting Recommendations and Endorsements:

LinkedIn's portfolio feature is even more powerful when combined with endorsements and recommendations from colleagues, clients, or supervisors. Encourage individuals who have worked closely with you to provide feedback on your portfolio items. Positive testimonials add credibility and validate your skills and achievements to potential employers.

vii. Optimizing Your Portfolio for Search:

Ensure that your portfolio is discoverable by optimizing your profile and portfolio content for relevant keywords. Conduct thorough research on industry-specific terms and incorporate them strategically into your descriptions and titles. This will increase the visibility of your work when recruiters or hiring managers search for candidates with specific skills or experiences.

viii. Promoting Your Portfolio:

Maximize the impact of your portfolio by promoting it proactively. Share your portfolio items through LinkedIn posts, groups, or articles to increase exposure and engage with your network. Actively participate in relevant discussions or forums to demonstrate your expertise and provide value to others in your industry.

Overall, LinkedIn's portfolio feature offers a valuable opportunity to showcase your work and strengthen your professional brand. By carefully selecting and presenting your best projects, providing context and descriptions, demonstrating diversity and updating regularly, and leveraging multimedia formats, you can effectively utilize this feature to make a strong impression on potential employers and clients.

Remember, LinkedIn's portfolio feature is not just a place to showcase your work; it's an opportunity to tell your professional story and demonstrate your expertise. Take the time to curate a collection of your best projects that align with your career goals and target audience. By investing in this aspect of your LinkedIn profile, you can stand out from the competition and increase your chances of landing the job or attracting the right clients.

So, start exploring LinkedIn's portfolio feature today, gather your most compelling work samples, and present them in an engaging and visually appealing manner. By leveraging this powerful tool, you can elevate your professional brand, establish credibility, and create more opportunities for career growth and success.

4.4 Publishing articles and sharing valuable content

Publishing articles and sharing valuable content are crucial aspects of building a strong professional presence on LinkedIn. In this section, I will provide valuable insights on how to effectively publish articles and share content to enhance your personal brand and attract job opportunities.

Here's a comprehensive guide:

★ Define Your Content Strategy:

Before you start publishing articles, it's essential to establish a clear content strategy. Identify your target audience, understand their needs, and determine the topics that align with your expertise. Consider the industry you're targeting and the skills you want to highlight. Developing a content strategy will help you stay focused and consistent in your publishing efforts.

★ Create Engaging and Relevant Content:

To stand out on LinkedIn, your content should be engaging, relevant, and valuable to your audience. Write articles that provide insights, actionable tips, or thought-provoking perspectives. Consider sharing success stories, lessons learned, industry trends, or expert opinions.

Use a conversational tone, include personal anecdotes, and present information in a well-structured and easily digestible format.

★ Optimize Your Articles for LinkedIn:

When publishing articles on LinkedIn, optimize them for maximum visibility. Pay attention to the title and opening paragraph, as they play a crucial role in capturing readers' attention. Incorporate relevant keywords throughout the article to improve searchability. Use headings, subheadings, and bullet points to enhance readability. Include visually appealing images or infographics to make your content more engaging.

★ Leverage LinkedIn Articles and Document Posts:

LinkedIn offers two primary formats for publishing content: LinkedIn Articles and Document Posts. LinkedIn Articles allow you to write long-form content directly on the platform, while Document Posts enable you to upload PDFs, presentations, or other documents. Experiment with both formats to diversify your content and cater to different preferences. However, ensure your content is well-organized and visually appealing regardless of the format you choose.

★ Engage with Your Audience:

Building a strong professional network involves engaging with your audience. Respond to comments on your articles, thank readers for their insights, and encourage discussions. Engage with other relevant articles by liking, commenting, and sharing them. Actively participate in industry-specific groups and contribute meaningful insights. Regularly monitor your notifications and engage with your connections to foster relationships and expand your network.

★ Share Valuable Content from Others:

While publishing your own articles is important, sharing valuable content from others also demonstrates your industry knowledge and generosity. Curate and share articles, blog posts, or news relevant to your field. When sharing, provide your insights or ask thoughtful questions to spark conversations. This not only enriches your network but also positions you as a valuable resource and increases your visibility.

★ Promote Your Content:

To maximize the reach of your articles and shared content, promote them effectively. Share your articles on other social media platforms, embed them in your personal website or blog, and include them in your email signature.

Use relevant hashtags to increase visibility within LinkedIn's ecosystem. Engage with LinkedIn influencers or thought leaders by mentioning them in your content or sharing their articles, which can help you gain exposure to their followers.

★ Measure and Adapt:

Monitor the performance of your published articles and shared content. LinkedIn provides analytics that offer insights into views, engagement, and the demographics of your audience. Pay attention to the topics, formats, and types of content that resonate the most with your audience. Based on these insights, adapt your content strategy to optimize your engagement and attract the attention of potential employers.

By following these guidelines and consistently publishing valuable content on LinkedIn, you can establish yourself as a knowledgeable professional and increase your visibility within your industry. Remember to maintain professionalism, be authentic, and stay engaged with your network.

4.5 Endorsements and Recommendations

Endorsements and recommendations play a crucial role in enhancing your professional profile on LinkedIn. They serve as valuable social proof of your skills, expertise, and work performance, making them essential components of your job search strategy. Let's delve into the details of endorsements and recommendations and explore how they can positively impact your career on LinkedIn.

Endorsements:

Endorsements are a quick and easy way for your connections to vouch for your skills and expertise. When someone endorses you for a particular skill, it means they believe you possess that skill and are proficient in it. Endorsements are displayed prominently on your profile, creating a snapshot of your professional strengths. Here's why endorsements matter:

a. **Visibility and Credibility**: Endorsements increase your visibility on LinkedIn and make you more discoverable by recruiters and potential employers. When you have a substantial number of endorsements for specific skills, it establishes credibility and validates your proficiency in those areas.

b. **Skill Verification**: Endorsements provide a level of skill verification. When a prospective employer or client views your profile and sees numerous endorsements for relevant skills, it reassures them that you possess the expertise they are seeking.

c. **Networking Opportunities**: Endorsements can also lead to new networking opportunities. When your connections endorse you, their network becomes aware of your skills, potentially expanding your reach and opening doors to new connections and opportunities.

To maximize the impact of endorsements, it's important to maintain an up-to-date skills section on your profile. List the skills that are most relevant to your desired job or industry. Actively engage with your network, endorse their skills, and kindly request endorsements in return. Remember to reciprocate the support to build strong professional relationships.

Recommendations:

Recommendations go beyond a simple endorsement; they are personalized testimonials that highlight your professional qualities and contributions. Recommendations are typically written by colleagues, supervisors, clients, or other individuals who have worked closely with you. Here's why recommendations are valuable:

a. **Detailed Insights**: Recommendations provide more in-depth insights into your work ethic, abilities, and accomplishments. They can offer specific examples of projects you've successfully completed, your teamwork skills, leadership qualities, and other commendable attributes. These detailed testimonials can have a powerful impact on potential employers.

b. **Trust and Authenticity**: Recommendations carry a high level of trust and authenticity. A genuine recommendation from a credible source can significantly influence the perception of your professional capabilities. Hiring managers and recruiters often place great value on recommendations as they provide a third-party perspective on your skills and character.

c. **Competitive Edge**: Recommendations give you a competitive edge in the job market. When competing with other candidates who have similar qualifications, having strong recommendations can make you stand out and increase your chances of securing an interview or job offer.

To gather recommendations effectively, reach out to individuals with whom you have a strong professional rapport. Consider asking colleagues, supervisors, mentors, or clients who can speak to your work performance and character.

Personalize your request by reminding them of specific projects or experiences you shared, making it easier for them to recall your contributions.

Remember to express your gratitude when someone provides a recommendation or endorsement. A thoughtful thank-you message shows appreciation and strengthens your professional relationships.

Overall, endorsements and recommendations on LinkedIn are powerful tools that enhance your professional credibility, visibility, and networking opportunities. Actively seek endorsements from your connections by endorsing their skills, and politely request recommendations from individuals who can provide detailed and positive testimonials about your work. By leveraging these features effectively, you can strengthen your profile and boost your chances of success in your job search endeavors.

4.6 Leveraging LinkedIn's job posting feature for recruiters

LinkedIn's job posting feature is a powerful tool that recruiters can leverage to effectively connect with potential candidates and streamline the hiring process. With millions of professionals actively using LinkedIn, posting jobs on this platform can significantly increase visibility and attract top talent.

In this section, I will provide an extensive overview of how recruiters can effectively leverage LinkedIn's job posting feature to enhance their hiring efforts.

★ Creating a Compelling Job Posting:

To attract qualified candidates, it is essential to create a compelling and informative job posting. Start by writing a concise and engaging job title that accurately reflects the position. Use relevant keywords and industry-specific terms to make the job posting more searchable. Provide a clear and detailed job description, outlining the responsibilities, qualifications, and any specific requirements. Highlight the unique aspects of the role and your company's culture to make it more appealing to potential candidates.

★ Utilizing LinkedIn's Targeting Options:

LinkedIn offers various targeting options to help recruiters reach their desired audience effectively. Take advantage of these options to ensure your job posting reaches the right professionals. You can target specific locations, industries, job functions, and experience levels. Additionally, you can refine your targeting further by specifying the company size, skills, and educational background of the ideal candidates. By utilizing these targeting options, you can maximize the visibility of your job posting to the most relevant audience i.e this increases the likelihood of attracting candidates with the desired skills and experience.

★ Showcasing the Company's Brand:

LinkedIn's job posting feature allows recruiters to showcase their company's brand and culture. Take advantage of this opportunity by providing a detailed company description and highlighting your organization's mission, values, and unique selling points. Include employee testimonials, photos, and videos to give candidates a glimpse into your company's work environment and culture. This helps create a strong employer brand and attracts candidates who align with your company's values.

★ **Engaging Visuals**:

LinkedIn allows you to include images, videos, and other multimedia elements in your job postings. Use this feature to showcase your workplace, team, or company events. Visual content can make your job post more engaging and help candidates envision themselves working for your organization.

★ **Leveraging Employee Referrals:**

LinkedIn's job posting feature integrates seamlessly with employee referral programs, making it easier for recruiters to leverage their employees' networks. Encourage your current employees to share job postings with their connections and offer incentives for successful referrals. By tapping into your employees' networks, you can reach a wider audience of qualified candidates who are more likely to be a good fit for your company.

★ **Active Promotion on LinkedIn**:

LinkedIn provides various tools for promoting job postings beyond the initial listing. Consider sponsoring your job posts to increase their visibility in candidates' feeds and search results. Additionally, join relevant LinkedIn groups and communities to share your job openings and engage with professionals who might be interested.

★ Engaging with Candidates:

Once you start receiving applications and inquiries, it is crucial to promptly engage with candidates. Respond to messages, acknowledge applications, and provide updates on the hiring process. LinkedIn's messaging feature enables recruiters to have direct conversations with candidates, allowing for efficient communication and a personalized candidate experience. Engaging with candidates in a timely and professional manner enhances your employer brand and fosters positive relationships with potential hires.

★ Leveraging LinkedIn's Talent Solutions:

LinkedIn offers additional tools and features through its Talent Solutions package to further enhance your job posting efforts. Features such as InMail messaging, candidate management features, advanced search filters, and talent analytics provide recruiters with more in-depth insights and capabilities to connect with candidates. Explore these options to enhance your recruitment efforts and gain a competitive edge in your recruitment efforts.

★ Streamlined Application Process:

Ensure that the application process is simple and user-friendly. A complex or time-consuming application process can discourage potential candidates from applying.

Use LinkedIn's built-in Easy Apply feature, which allows candidates to submit their applications with just a few clicks.

★ Analyzing Performance and Optimizing:

LinkedIn provides robust analytics and reporting features that allow recruiters to measure the performance of their job postings. Track metrics such as the number of views, clicks, and applications to assess the effectiveness of your job posting strategy. Use these insights to optimize future postings, refine targeting options, and make data-driven decisions to attract the right candidates.

By leveraging LinkedIn's job posting feature effectively, recruiters can expand their reach, attract top talent, and streamline the hiring process. Combining compelling job descriptions, targeted audience selection, optimized keywords, visual content, employee advocacy, active promotion, a streamlined application process, and the use of LinkedIn Recruiter, recruiters can maximize the potential of LinkedIn as a recruitment platform.

Chapter 5: Engaging Effectively on LinkedIn

5.1 Understanding LinkedIn etiquette

LinkedIn is a powerful professional networking platform that allows individuals to connect, engage, and build relationships with other professionals in various industries. To make the most out of LinkedIn and present yourself in a professional manner, it is essential to understand and follow proper LinkedIn etiquette. Here, we will delve into the key aspects of LinkedIn etiquette to help you navigate the platform effectively.

★ **Creating a Complete Profile:**

Your LinkedIn profile serves as your digital resume and is the first impression you make on others. It is crucial to create a comprehensive and professional profile that showcases your skills, experience, and accomplishments. Include a clear and recent profile picture, a compelling headline, and a well-written summary that highlights your expertise.

★ **Personalize Connection Requests:**

When sending connection requests, take the time to personalize each message. Avoid generic requests and demonstrate genuine interest in connecting with the individual.

Mention a shared interest or explain why you believe connecting would be beneficial for both parties. Personalized connection requests are more likely to be accepted.

★ Engaging in Meaningful Interactions:

LinkedIn is a platform for professional networking, so it's important to engage in meaningful interactions. When commenting on posts or participating in group discussions, provide thoughtful insights and contribute value to the conversation. Avoid spamming or self-promotion, as it can be seen as unprofessional behavior.

★ Sending Professional Messages:

When sending messages to your connections, maintain a professional tone and keep your messages concise and clear. Be respectful of the recipient's time and avoid using LinkedIn messaging for personal or unrelated matters. If you are reaching out to someone for the first time, briefly introduce yourself and explain the purpose of your message.

★ Endorsing and Recommending Others:

LinkedIn allows you to endorse the skills of your connections and provide recommendations. Endorsements should be genuine and based on your personal knowledge of the person's skills. When writing recommendations, be specific, highlight their strengths, and provide examples of their work. Requesting endorsements and recommendations should be done sparingly and only when you have a genuine professional relationship with the person.

★ Sharing Relevant and Valuable Content:

LinkedIn is a platform for sharing professional content and industry insights. When sharing articles, blog posts, or other content, ensure that it is relevant to your connections and adds value to their professional lives. Use a professional tone and provide your own insights or thoughts to accompany the shared content. Avoid sharing controversial or overly personal content that may alienate or offend others.

★ Managing Connection Requests and Invitations:

It is important to manage your connection requests and invitations effectively. Accept connection requests from individuals you know or those who have personalized their requests. If you receive requests from individuals you don't know, evaluate their profiles and mutual connections before accepting. Be polite when declining requests, providing a brief explanation if necessary.

★ Professionalism in Job Searches:

LinkedIn is a valuable tool for job seekers, but it's important to maintain professionalism throughout the job search process. Avoid publicly criticizing current or past employers, and be cautious when discussing confidential information. Use LinkedIn's private messaging feature for sensitive discussions related to job opportunities.

★ Respecting Privacy and Boundaries:

Respect the privacy and boundaries of your connections on LinkedIn. Avoid spamming or repeatedly reaching out to connections who have not responded or shown interest. Be mindful of sharing confidential information and always seek permission before sharing someone else's content or work.

★ Regular Engagement and Active Networking:

To make the most of LinkedIn, engage regularly with your connections and the content they share. Like, comment, and share posts that align with your professional interests. Actively participate in relevant groups and contribute to discussions. Building and nurturing relationships through consistent engagement is key to leveraging LinkedIn effectively.

★ Acknowledging Connection Requests and Messages:

It is courteous to promptly acknowledge connection requests and messages you receive on LinkedIn. Even if you cannot respond immediately, take the time to acknowledge the request or message and let the person know that you will get back to them soon. Ignoring or delaying responses can give off a negative impression and hinder relationship-building efforts.

By understanding and adhering to these LinkedIn etiquette guidelines, you can establish a professional online presence, build meaningful connections, and enhance your professional reputation on LinkedIn.

5.2 Sharing relevant and engaging content

When it comes to sharing content on LinkedIn, it's important to focus on providing value to your professional network by sharing relevant and engaging content.

Here are some key points to consider:

Understand your audience: Before sharing any content, take the time to understand your LinkedIn network and their interests. Identify the industries they belong to, their job roles, and the topics they engage with most. This will help you tailor your content to their preferences and ensure it resonates with them.

Share industry insights: LinkedIn is a professional networking platform where individuals seek to expand their knowledge and stay up-to-date with industry trends. Share insightful articles, reports, or studies relevant to your field. Provide your own commentary or ask thought-provoking questions to encourage discussions.

Create original content: Stand out from the crowd by creating your own content. Write articles, share case studies, or create videos that offer unique insights or perspectives. This establishes you as a thought leader and can help you build your personal brand on LinkedIn.

Engage with others' content: Sharing content isn't just about broadcasting your own ideas; it's also about building relationships and engaging with others. Like, comment, and share content from your network that you find interesting or valuable. This helps you nurture professional connections and encourages reciprocity.

Use visuals effectively: Visual content tends to capture attention and drive engagement. When sharing articles or updates, include relevant images, infographics, or videos to make your content more appealing. Ensure that visuals are high-quality and align with the message you want to convey.

Leverage LinkedIn features: LinkedIn offers various features to enhance your content-sharing strategy. Consider using hashtags to increase discoverability, tag relevant individuals or companies in your posts to increase visibility, and participate in LinkedIn groups or communities to engage with a targeted audience.

Monitor and analyze performance: Regularly monitor the performance of your shared content to understand what resonates with your network. LinkedIn provides analytics that show metrics such as views, likes, comments, and shares. Use this data to refine your content strategy and focus on topics that generate the most engagement.

Be consistent and reliable: To build credibility and maintain engagement, it's important to be consistent with your content sharing. Develop a posting schedule that aligns with your audience's preferences and stick to it. Regularly share valuable content to establish yourself as a reliable source of information.

Remember, sharing relevant and engaging content on LinkedIn is not just about self-promotion. It's about fostering meaningful connections, providing value to your network, and positioning yourself as a knowledgeable professional. By focusing on these principles, you can effectively share content that resonates with your audience and contributes to your professional growth.

5.3 Commenting and engaging in discussions

Commenting and engaging in discussions on LinkedIn is an effective way to build your professional network, establish thought leadership, and enhance your personal brand.

Here's an extensive explanation on how to effectively comment and engage in discussions on LinkedIn:

* **Be Relevant**: When commenting on LinkedIn posts, ensure that your comments are relevant to the topic at hand. Read the post carefully and understand its context before sharing your thoughts. This demonstrates your expertise and adds value to the conversation.

* **Add Value**: Instead of leaving generic comments like "Great post!" or "I agree," strive to provide meaningful insights or ask thought-provoking questions. Share your expertise, share examples or relevant anecdotes, and offer unique perspectives that contribute to the discussion. This helps you stand out and positions you as a valuable contributor.

★ **Be Respectful and Professional:** LinkedIn is a professional platform, so maintain a respectful and professional tone in your comments. Even if you disagree with someone's opinion, express your differing viewpoint in a courteous manner. Engage in constructive debates and avoid personal attacks or offensive language. Remember, your comments are a reflection of your professional reputation.

★ **Engage with Others**: LinkedIn is a networking platform, so make an effort to engage with others' comments as well. Reply to comments on your own posts and acknowledge the contributions of others by liking or replying to their comments. This fosters a sense of community and encourages further discussion.

★ **Follow Up**: If someone responds to your comment or asks you a question, make sure to respond in a timely manner. This demonstrates your active engagement and willingness to continue the conversation. Promptly addressing queries or engaging in further discussions can help deepen your professional connections.

★ **Use Mention and Hashtags**: To direct your comments to specific individuals or groups, use the @mention feature.

This notifies the person or group you mention and increases the likelihood of their engagement. Additionally, incorporating relevant hashtags in your comments can help your comments reach a wider audience interested in the topic.

★ **Stay Consistent**: Regularly engage in discussions on LinkedIn to maintain a consistent presence. Set aside dedicated time to read and comment on relevant posts, and consider joining groups or following hashtags that align with your professional interests. Consistency demonstrates your commitment to professional networking and helps you stay top of mind within your industry.

★ **Monitor Notifications**: LinkedIn provides notification settings that allow you to receive alerts when someone responds to your comments or mentions you. Stay on top of these notifications and respond promptly. This demonstrates your active engagement and encourages further interactions.

By following these practices, you can effectively comment and engage in discussions on LinkedIn, expand your professional network, and establish yourself as a thought leader within your industry. Remember to always be professional, respectful, and provide valuable insights to maximize the impact of your engagement efforts.

5.4 Using hashtags effectively

Using hashtags effectively on LinkedIn can significantly enhance your visibility and engagement with your target audience. Here's a detailed explanation of how to use hashtags effectively on the platform:

★ **Research relevant hashtags**: Begin by researching and identifying relevant hashtags in your industry or niche. Look for popular and trending hashtags that are frequently used by professionals in your field. LinkedIn's search bar and content recommendations can help you discover relevant hashtags.

★ **Mix broad and specific hashtags**: When selecting hashtags, strike a balance between broad and specific ones. Broad hashtags like #business or #marketing can expose your content to a larger audience, while specific hashtags like #digitalmarketingstrategy or #leadershipdevelopment can help you reach a more targeted audience.

★ **Stay focused on your content**: Ensure that the hashtags you use accurately reflect the content of your post. Avoid using irrelevant or misleading hashtags, as this can lead to disengagement or negative reactions from users.

Aligning your hashtags with your content will attract the right audience and increase the chances of meaningful interactions.

★ **Use industry-specific hashtags**: Incorporate industry-specific hashtags that are commonly used by professionals in your field. These hashtags help you connect with like-minded individuals, industry experts, and potential employers or clients. Industry-specific hashtags can also establish your credibility and expertise within your niche.

★ **Include location-based hashtags:** If your content is relevant to a specific location, consider using location-based hashtags. For example, if you're sharing insights about the tech industry in San Francisco, include hashtags like #SanFranciscoTech or #SiliconValley. This will help you connect with professionals in that area and boost your visibility within the local community.

★ **Research hashtag popularity**: Evaluate the popularity and engagement level of hashtags before incorporating them into your content. LinkedIn displays the number of followers for each hashtag, indicating the approximate audience size.

Use a combination of popular and niche hashtags to maximize reach and engagement.

★ **Create branded hashtags**: Building your own branded hashtags can help establish your unique identity and encourage others to engage with your content. Branded hashtags should be concise, easy to remember, and reflect your brand or professional persona. Encourage your network to use your branded hashtags when discussing topics related to your brand or industry.

★ **Engage with hashtag communities:** LinkedIn has various groups and communities centered around specific hashtags. Engaging with these communities by commenting, liking, and sharing content can boost your visibility and expand your professional network. It's important to provide valuable insights and participate in meaningful discussions to establish yourself as an active and knowledgeable professional.

★ **Monitor and analyze performance**: Regularly monitor the performance of your posts with different hashtags. LinkedIn provides insights on how many views, likes, comments, and shares your content receives.

Analyzing this data will help you identify which hashtags are most effective in reaching your target audience and generating engagement.

★ **Stay updated and adapt:** Stay up-to-date with industry trends, news, and popular hashtags. LinkedIn's content recommendations and exploring relevant profiles in your industry can help you discover new hashtags to incorporate into your strategy. Continuously adapt your hashtag usage based on the changing dynamics of your industry and audience preferences.

Remember, using hashtags effectively on LinkedIn requires a strategic approach. By researching, selecting, and using relevant hashtags, you can increase your visibility, connect with the right audience, and build your professional brand on the platform.

5.5 Participating in LinkedIn events and webinars

Participating in LinkedIn events and webinars can be a valuable strategy to enhance your professional presence, network with industry experts, gain insights, and showcase your expertise.

Here's an extensive explanation on how to make the most of these opportunities:

1. Finding Events and Webinars:

- Explore the "Events" tab on LinkedIn or use the search bar to find relevant events and webinars.
- Filter your search based on location, industry, date, or specific topics of interest.
- Follow company pages and influencers in your field to stay updated on their events.

2. Choosing the Right Events and Webinars:

- Select events and webinars that align with your professional goals, interests, and industry.
- Consider the event's reputation, organizer, speakers, and the topics covered.

- Read event descriptions, agendas, and attendee profiles to ensure relevance.

3. Engaging Before the Event:

- Review the event details, including the agenda and speakers' profiles, to familiarize yourself with the content and participants.
- Connect with other attendees or speakers prior to the event through LinkedIn messages or by engaging with their content.
- Share the event or webinar on your LinkedIn feed to notify your network and generate interest.

4. Active Participation During the Event:

- Be present and engaged during the event or webinar. Take notes, ask questions, and participate in polls or discussions.
- Utilize the chat or Q&A features to interact with speakers, fellow attendees, and organizers.
- Show appreciation by thanking the speakers or organizers for their insights or by sharing valuable takeaways on LinkedIn.

5. Networking Opportunities:

- Take advantage of networking opportunities offered during the event, such as virtual breakout sessions, networking lounges, or LinkedIn groups associated with the event.
- Connect with speakers and participants who share similar interests or expertise.
- Follow up with new connections after the event by sending personalized LinkedIn connection requests or messages.

6. Sharing Insights and Takeaways:

- Share valuable insights, key learnings, or interesting takeaways from the event on your LinkedIn feed.
- Tag the event organizers, speakers, or fellow attendees in your posts to extend the conversation and increase visibility.
- Use relevant hashtags and mention any relevant companies or industry influencers to reach a broader audience.

7. Leveraging Recorded Content:

- If the event or webinar is recorded and made available afterward, revisit the content to reinforce your learning or capture missed sessions.
- Share noteworthy recordings with your network, adding your thoughts or key points to start conversations.

8. Growing Your Influence:

- Consider hosting your own LinkedIn event or webinar to showcase your expertise and build your personal brand.
- Apply to be a speaker or panelist at relevant events to increase your visibility and credibility.
- Create and share engaging content related to the event topics to position yourself as a thought leader.

Remember, active and thoughtful participation in LinkedIn events and webinars can help you expand your professional network, stay updated on industry trends, and establish yourself as a knowledgeable professional in your field.

Chapter 6: Harnessing the Power of LinkedIn Analytics

6.1 Tracking profile views and engagement

Tracking profile views and engagement on LinkedIn is crucial for professionals who want to gain insights into their online presence and measure the effectiveness of their networking and personal branding efforts. LinkedIn offers various features and tools to help users track and analyze their profile views and engagement metrics.

Profile Views:

LinkedIn allows users to see the number of times their profile has been viewed within a specific time frame. This feature provides valuable information about the visibility and reach of your profile. To access this data, navigate to your LinkedIn profile and locate the "Who viewed your profile" section. Here, you can see the total number of profile views and get a breakdown of who has viewed your profile, including their job titles, industries, and locations.

Profile Engagement:

Beyond profile views, LinkedIn also provides metrics related to engagement with your profile content. These metrics include likes, comments, and shares on your posts, as well as the number of times your articles, documents, and media have been viewed or interacted with.

To monitor engagement, visit the "Activity" tab on your LinkedIn profile. This section displays a summary of your recent posts, articles, and interactions. Clicking on a specific post or article will provide more detailed engagement metrics, such as the number of views, likes, comments, and shares.

In addition to these built-in analytics features, LinkedIn also offers Premium subscriptions, such as LinkedIn Premium and Sales Navigator, which provide enhanced profile analytics and additional insights. Premium subscribers can access more detailed data on who has viewed their profile, including the ability to view all profile viewers within a specific time frame and see how their profile views compare to other professionals in their industry or network.

Tracking profile views and engagement on LinkedIn is valuable for several reasons:

- Personal Branding: By monitoring profile views, you can assess how effectively you are promoting your personal brand and increasing your visibility within your professional network.

- Networking: Knowing who has viewed your profile allows you to identify potential connections and reach out to individuals who have shown interest in your background and expertise.

- Content Strategy: Tracking engagement metrics helps you understand which types of content resonate with your audience and can inform your content strategy. By analyzing the number of views, likes, comments, and shares, you can identify trends and preferences among your connections.

- Job Search: If you are actively searching for job opportunities, tracking profile views can help you gauge the level of interest from recruiters and hiring managers. It can also provide insights into which companies or industries are engaging with your profile.

6.2 Analyzing post-performance and audience insights

Analyzing post-performance and audience insights on LinkedIn is crucial for understanding the effectiveness of your content and optimizing your strategy. It provides valuable data and metrics that help you make informed decisions to improve your engagement and reach your target audience more effectively.

Here are some key aspects to consider when analyzing post-performance and audience insights on LinkedIn:

* ★ **Reach and Impressions**: These metrics show how many LinkedIn users have seen your post (reach) and how many times it has been displayed (impressions). Analyzing these numbers helps you gauge the visibility of your content and its potential reach within the platform.

* ★ **Engagement Metrics**: LinkedIn provides various engagement metrics, including likes, comments, and shares. These metrics indicate how well your content resonates with your audience. By analyzing the types and quantity of engagements, you can identify which posts are generating the most interest and engagement.

★ **Click-through Rates (CTR)**: CTR measures the percentage of users who clicked on a link within your post, leading them to another destination, such as your website or a landing page. Analyzing CTR helps you evaluate the effectiveness of your call-to-action (CTA) and the overall interest your audience has in the content you are sharing.

★ **Follower Demographics**: LinkedIn's audience insights provide valuable information about your followers, such as their location, industry, job function, and seniority level. Understanding these demographics helps you tailor your content to align with your target audience's interests and preferences.

★ **Post Timing and Frequency**: Analyzing the performance of your posts over time helps you identify patterns and trends. You can determine the best days and times to post content to maximize visibility and engagement. Additionally, analyzing the frequency of your posts allows you to find the optimal balance between staying top-of-mind and avoiding overwhelming your audience.

★ **Content Analysis**: By analyzing the types of content that perform well on LinkedIn, you can refine your content strategy. Identify the topics, formats, and themes that generate the most engagement and adjust your future content accordingly.

★ **A/B Testing**: Experimentation is key to optimizing your LinkedIn strategy. Conducting A/B tests involves creating variations of your content (e.g., different headlines, images, or formats) and comparing their performance. This helps you understand what resonates best with your audience and fine-tune your approach.

To access these insights on LinkedIn, you can utilize the platform's built-in analytics tools or use third-party social media management tools that provide more in-depth analytics and reporting capabilities. Regularly reviewing and analyzing these metrics and insights will help you make data-driven decisions, refine your content strategy, and achieve better results on LinkedIn.

6.3 Using data to optimize your LinkedIn strategy

Data plays a crucial role in understanding the performance of your LinkedIn activities and making informed decisions to achieve your goals.

Here are some key steps to utilize data effectively:

★ **Define your objectives**: Start by clearly defining your objectives. Whether it's increasing brand visibility, generating leads, or recruiting talent, having well-defined goals will guide your data analysis efforts.

★ **Track relevant metrics**: LinkedIn provides a range of metrics to track your performance. Important metrics include profile views, post engagement (likes, comments, shares), click-through rates, follower growth, and conversion rates. Identify the metrics that align with your objectives and regularly track them.

★ **Utilize LinkedIn Analytics**: LinkedIn offers a built-in analytics platform called LinkedIn Page Analytics and LinkedIn Campaign Manager. These tools provide detailed data on various aspects of your LinkedIn presence, such as audience demographics, engagement levels, and content performance.

Explore these analytics to gain valuable insights into your audience and content strategy.

★ **Analyze engagement patterns**: Look for patterns in the type of content that receives the most engagement. Identify the topics, formats, and posting times that resonate well with your audience. Use this information to optimize your content strategy and create more engaging posts.

★ **Experiment and iterate**: Use A/B testing to experiment with different variations of your content and measure their performance. Test different headlines, visuals, calls-to-action, and formats to identify the most effective elements for your audience. Continuously iterate and refine your strategy based on data-driven insights.

★ **Identify top-performing content**: Analyze the content that performs exceptionally well and try to understand the reasons behind its success. It could be due to its relevance, uniqueness, or the value it provides to your audience. Replicate and adapt successful content to maintain consistency and drive engagement.

★ **Monitor competitor activity**: Keep an eye on your competitors' LinkedIn presence and analyze their strategies. Identify what works well for them and learn from their successes. Use data to benchmark your performance against industry peers and make data-informed decisions to stay competitive.

★ **Optimize your profile**: Leverage data to optimize your LinkedIn profile. Analyze the keywords and phrases that resonate with your audience and incorporate them into your profile, headline, and summary. Pay attention to the sections that receive the most views and engagement and make necessary improvements.

★ **Stay informed with industry trends**: Stay updated with the latest trends and changes on LinkedIn. Regularly review LinkedIn's blog, participate in relevant LinkedIn groups, and follow thought leaders in your industry. Understanding the evolving landscape will help you adapt your strategy and take advantage of new opportunities.

★ **Monitor and adapt:** Continuously monitor your performance metrics and adjust your strategy accordingly. Identify areas of improvement, experiment with new approaches, and learn from your data to optimize your LinkedIn strategy over time.

Remember, data is a powerful tool, but it's important to interpret it in the context of your specific goals and target audience. By consistently analyzing data, making data-driven decisions, and adapting your strategy, you can optimize your LinkedIn presence and achieve better results.

Chapter 7: Advanced LinkedIn Strategies

7.1 Building a personal brand on LinkedIn

Building a personal brand on LinkedIn is essential for professionals who want to establish their expertise, expand their network, and enhance their career opportunities.

Here are key steps to effectively build your personal brand on LinkedIn:

★ **Define your personal brand**: Start by identifying your unique value proposition and what sets you apart from others in your field. Consider your skills, experience, and passion. Define your professional goals and target audience. This clarity will guide your content creation and engagement strategies.

★ **Optimize your LinkedIn profile**: Your LinkedIn profile serves as your online resume and professional identity. Ensure your profile picture is professional and your headline succinctly highlights your expertise. Craft a compelling summary that showcases your skills and achievements. Add relevant keywords to improve searchability. Complete all sections, including education, work experience, and certifications.

★ **Engage with relevant content**: Regularly engage with relevant content by liking, commenting, and sharing. This demonstrates your expertise and interests. Share valuable insights, industry news, and thought leadership articles to position yourself as a knowledgeable professional. Engaging with others' content helps you build connections and establish relationships with like-minded individuals.

★ **Create original content**: Sharing original content is a powerful way to showcase your expertise and build your personal brand. Write articles, publish posts, or create videos that provide value to your target audience. Focus on topics related to your industry, offer insights, and share practical tips. Be consistent in your content creation to stay top-of-mind with your network.

★ **Build a professional network**: Connect with professionals in your industry, colleagues, former classmates, and people you meet at events. Personalize your connection requests to make a genuine connection. Join LinkedIn Groups related to your field to engage with professionals and share your expertise. Actively participate in discussions and offer helpful insights.

★ **Request and give endorsements and recommendations**: Request endorsements for your skills from colleagues and connections who can vouch for your expertise. Additionally, request recommendations from mentors, supervisors, or clients who can provide testimonials on your work. Offer endorsements and recommendations to others when you can genuinely vouch for their skills and expertise.

★ **Participate in LinkedIn communities**: Engage in LinkedIn communities such as industry-specific groups, professional forums, or LinkedIn Live events. This allows you to connect with like-minded professionals, expand your network, and contribute to relevant conversations. Sharing your insights and expertise in these communities can enhance your visibility and credibility.

★ **Leverage LinkedIn features**: Utilize LinkedIn features such as LinkedIn Live, LinkedIn Stories, and LinkedIn Events to engage with your audience in real-time, share updates, and promote webinars or events you are hosting or attending. These features can help you stand out and reach a broader audience.

★ **Monitor and analyze your performance**: Regularly review your LinkedIn analytics to understand the impact of your content and engagement efforts. Pay attention to metrics like profile views, post reach, engagement rate, and connection growth. Analyzing your performance helps you identify what strategies work best and make adjustments accordingly.

★ **Be authentic and consistent**: Authenticity is key when building your personal brand. Be true to yourself and showcase your unique personality. Consistency is also crucial, both in terms of posting regularly and maintaining a consistent professional image. Building a personal brand takes time and effort, so remain patient and persistent.

By following these steps, you can effectively build your personal brand on LinkedIn and establish yourself as a reputable professional in your industry, creating new opportunities for career growth and networking.

7.2 Leveraging LinkedIn for thought leadership

Leveraging LinkedIn for thought leadership is an effective strategy for establishing yourself as a trusted authority in your industry and gaining visibility among professionals in your field. LinkedIn provides a platform with over 774 million members, making it an ideal place to showcase your expertise, share valuable insights, and build a network of like-minded professionals.

Here are some key steps to effectively leverage LinkedIn for thought leadership:

★ Optimize your LinkedIn profile: Create a professional and compelling profile that highlights your expertise, achievements, and relevant industry experience. Use a high-quality headshot, craft a concise and engaging headline, and optimize your summary and work experience sections with relevant keywords.

★ Consistent content creation: Regularly publish high-quality and insightful content on LinkedIn to establish yourself as a thought leader. Share industry trends, analysis, case studies, and practical tips that demonstrate your expertise and provide value to your audience. Aim for a mix of long-form articles, short posts, and multimedia content like videos or infographics.

★ Engage with your network: Thought leadership is not just about broadcasting your own ideas, but also engaging in conversations and building relationships with others. Respond to comments on your posts, engage in discussions, and provide thoughtful insights on other people's content. This helps you expand your network and establish yourself as a trusted and approachable expert.

★ Join relevant groups: LinkedIn groups are a great way to connect with professionals in your industry or niche. Find and join groups that align with your expertise and actively participate in discussions. Share valuable insights, answer questions, and contribute to the community. This not only helps you showcase your thought leadership but also allows you to learn from others and stay updated on industry trends.

★ Utilize LinkedIn Pulse: LinkedIn Pulse is the platform's content publishing feature that allows you to share your articles and blog posts directly with your network and beyond. Leverage Pulse to amplify your reach and increase visibility. Optimize your Pulse articles with compelling headlines, relevant tags, and engaging visuals to attract more readers.

★ Utilize LinkedIn SlideShare: SlideShare is a popular presentation-sharing platform owned by LinkedIn. It provides an opportunity to share visually appealing and informative slideshows, infographics, and presentations that showcase your expertise. Create compelling SlideShare presentations that provide valuable insights and solutions to industry challenges.

★ Collaborate with others: Partnering with other thought leaders and industry influencers can help you expand your reach and credibility. Look for opportunities to collaborate on joint articles, podcasts, webinars, or speaking engagements. By associating yourself with respected experts in your field, you enhance your thought leadership presence and gain access to their networks.

★ Analyze and iterate: Regularly analyze the performance of your content and engagement metrics on LinkedIn. Pay attention to which types of posts and topics generate the most engagement and adjust your content strategy accordingly. Experiment with different formats, headlines, and topics to find what resonates best with your audience.

Remember, building thought leadership takes time and consistent effort. By leveraging LinkedIn's platform effectively, sharing valuable content, engaging with your network, and collaborating with others, you can establish yourself as a thought leader in your industry and make a lasting impact on your professional reputation.

7.3 Exploring LinkedIn advertising options

LinkedIn offers several advertising options that can help businesses reach their target audience and achieve their marketing goals. These options include:

* ★ **Sponsored Content**: This type of advertising appears directly in users' LinkedIn feeds. Businesses can promote their posts, articles, or multimedia content to a specific audience based on criteria such as job title, industry, location, and more. Sponsored content allows for engagement through likes, comments, and shares, increasing brand visibility and generating leads.

* ★ **Sponsored InMail**: With Sponsored InMail, businesses can send personalized messages directly to LinkedIn users' inboxes. These messages can include text, images, and call-to-action buttons. Sponsored InMail is a powerful tool for lead generation, event promotion, and driving conversions.

★ **Text Ads**: Text ads on LinkedIn are small, concise ads displayed on the right side of the LinkedIn desktop interface. They are typically used for promoting offers, driving traffic to websites or landing pages, and increasing brand awareness. Text ads can be targeted based on various demographic and professional criteria.

★ **Dynamic Ads**: Dynamic ads are personalized ads that appear on the right side of LinkedIn users' feeds. They can include a user's profile picture, name, and other relevant information, making them highly personalized and attention-grabbing. Dynamic ads are effective for driving engagement and increasing brand recognition.

★ **LinkedIn Video Ads**: Video ads on LinkedIn allow businesses to tell their story through engaging video content. These ads can be placed within the LinkedIn feed and autoplay as users scroll. Video ads are an excellent way to showcase products or services, highlight customer testimonials, and drive brand engagement.

★ **LinkedIn Lead Gen Forms**: This feature simplifies the lead generation process by allowing users to submit their contact information directly through LinkedIn ads. When a user clicks on a sponsored content or InMail ad, a pre-filled form appears, saving time and effort. LinkedIn Lead Gen Forms integrate seamlessly with various marketing automation platforms, making lead management more efficient.

★ **LinkedIn Display Ads**: Display ads on LinkedIn appear in various formats, including banner ads, text ads, and follower ads. These ads are displayed on LinkedIn partner websites, targeting specific audiences based on their LinkedIn profile information. Display ads are an effective way to increase brand exposure beyond the LinkedIn platform.

When exploring LinkedIn advertising options, it is important to define clear campaign objectives, identify the target audience, and allocate a budget accordingly. LinkedIn provides robust targeting capabilities that allow businesses to reach professionals based on job title, industry, company size, and more. Regular monitoring, testing, and optimization are key to ensuring the success of LinkedIn advertising campaigns.

7.4 Networking techniques for career growth

Networking plays a crucial role in expanding professional opportunities, building relationships, and enhancing your career. Here are some key techniques to consider:

★ **Establish a strong LinkedIn presence**: Create a compelling and professional LinkedIn profile that highlights your skills, experience, and achievements. Use a high-quality photo and craft a well-written summary. Regularly update your profile with relevant content, such as articles, industry insights, and accomplishments.

★ **Expand your network**: Actively connect with professionals in your field and related industries. Start by reaching out to colleagues, classmates, and former employers. Attend industry events, conferences, and seminars to meet new people. Join LinkedIn groups and engage in meaningful discussions.

★ **Personalize connection requests**: When sending connection requests, personalize them by mentioning how you found the person or why you're interested in connecting. This helps create a stronger initial connection and increases the likelihood of acceptance.

★ **Engage with others' content**: Like, comment, and share content posted by your connections to stay on their radar. Engaging with their content shows your interest and helps build relationships. Additionally, share valuable content from your own experiences and expertise to position yourself as a thought leader.

★ **Request informational interviews**: Reach out to professionals whose careers or organizations you admire and request a brief virtual or in-person informational interview. Prepare thoughtful questions and show genuine interest in learning from their experiences. These conversations can provide valuable insights and expand your network.

★ **Attend networking events**: Seek out local networking events, industry conferences, and meetups. These gatherings offer opportunities to connect with professionals face-to-face, exchange business cards, and build meaningful relationships.

★ **Offer assistance and provide value**: Be proactive in helping others. Offer your expertise, provide insights, or connect people who can benefit from each other. By adding value to your network, you increase the likelihood of reciprocity and strengthen professional relationships.

★ **Maintain regular communication**: Stay in touch with your connections through periodic messages, emails, or phone calls. Congratulate them on their achievements, share relevant resources, or simply check-in. Building and nurturing relationships is an ongoing process.

★ **Join relevant LinkedIn groups**: Engage in industry-specific LinkedIn groups where professionals share insights, ask questions, and seek advice. Participating in discussions allows you to establish your expertise and broaden your network.

★ **Attend webinars and virtual events**: In addition to in-person events, take advantage of virtual opportunities to connect with professionals worldwide. Webinars, online workshops, and virtual conferences offer platforms to learn, interact, and network with industry experts.

Remember, effective networking is not just about expanding your contacts, but also about building genuine relationships based on mutual trust and support. By implementing these techniques consistently, you can enhance your career growth potential and open doors to new opportunities.

7.5 Leveraging LinkedIn for business and entrepreneurship

LinkedIn is a powerful platform for business and entrepreneurship, offering a range of opportunities to connect with professionals, build brand visibility, and generate leads. Here are some key strategies to leverage LinkedIn effectively:

★ Optimize Your Profile: Create a professional and compelling profile that showcases your expertise, skills, and achievements. Use a high-quality headshot and write a concise yet engaging summary. Customize your URL, add relevant keywords, and highlight your accomplishments.

★ Expand Your Network: Connect with industry professionals, colleagues, clients, and influencers in your field. Personalize connection requests to make a positive impression. Join relevant LinkedIn groups and engage in discussions to build relationships and expand your network further.

★ Share Engaging Content: Regularly post valuable content related to your industry or niche. This can include articles, industry insights, success stories, or tips.

★ Share your expertise, be authentic, and aim to provide value to your audience. Use visuals, such as images or videos, to enhance engagement.

★ Engage with Others: Interact with your connections' content by liking, commenting, and sharing. This helps to foster relationships, increase visibility, and establish yourself as a thought leader. Respond promptly to messages and connection requests to maintain a proactive presence.

★ Publish Articles: LinkedIn's publishing platform allows you to showcase your expertise by writing long-form articles. Create in-depth content that addresses industry challenges, provides solutions, or offers valuable insights. This establishes credibility and attracts a wider audience.

★ Utilize LinkedIn Groups: Join and actively participate in relevant LinkedIn groups related to your industry or target audience. Contribute to discussions, share your expertise, and connect with like-minded professionals. This can help you gain visibility, establish authority, and find potential business opportunities.

★ Leverage LinkedIn Company Pages: If you have a business, create a LinkedIn company page to showcase your brand, products, and services. Share updates, job postings, and industry news. Encourage employees and customers to engage with your content, amplifying your reach.

★ Utilize LinkedIn Ads: Consider using LinkedIn's advertising platform to reach a specific target audience. LinkedIn offers various ad formats, such as sponsored content, text ads, and sponsored InMail. Define your target audience, set clear objectives, and monitor the performance of your ads to optimize results.

★ **Generate Leads**: Use LinkedIn's advanced search feature to find potential clients, partners, or investors. Narrow down your search based on specific criteria, such as industry, location, job title, or company size. Personalize your outreach messages and offer value when connecting with prospects.

★ **Network Offline**: LinkedIn is not limited to online interactions. Attend industry events, conferences, and seminars where you can meet professionals from your network in person. Strengthening online connections with face-to-face interactions can deepen relationships and open new business opportunities.

Chapter 8: Maintaining a Professional Online Presence

8.1 Managing privacy settings

LinkedIn offers various privacy settings to help you control the visibility of your profile and the information you share. By managing your privacy settings, you can ensure that your professional information is shared with the right audience and maintain a secure online presence. Here are some key aspects of managing privacy settings on LinkedIn:

★ **Profile Privacy**: You can control the visibility of your profile by adjusting the privacy settings. You have the option to make your profile public, visible to your connections only, or even more restricted to specific individuals. To access these settings, click on your profile picture in the top right corner, select "Settings & Privacy," and go to the "Privacy" tab.

★ **Public Profile**: LinkedIn allows you to create a public profile that is visible to users who are not connected to you. Within the privacy settings, you can choose what information is displayed on your public profile, such as your headline, summary, experience, and education.

Customizing this visibility can help you showcase the right information to potential employers or professional contacts.

★ **Activity Broadcasting**: LinkedIn provides options for broadcasting your activity on the platform. You can decide whether to share updates when you edit your profile, follow companies, join groups, or make recommendations. Adjusting these settings ensures that your network is informed about your activities according to your preference.

★ **Network Visibility**: LinkedIn enables you to control who can see your connections. You can choose to display your connections publicly, restrict visibility to your immediate connections, or hide them altogether. It's worth considering the balance between showcasing your professional network and maintaining privacy when configuring this setting.

★ **Search Engine Visibility**: LinkedIn allows you to determine whether your profile appears in search engine results. By default, your profile is visible to search engines. However, if you prefer to limit your visibility, you can switch off this option in the privacy settings.

★ **Communication Preferences**: LinkedIn offers control over how you receive communication from other members. You can manage settings related to invitations, messages, and notifications. These preferences can help you strike a balance between staying connected and avoiding excessive communication.

★ **Data Usage**: LinkedIn provides options to control how your data is used by the platform for personalized experiences, advertising, and third-party applications. Under the "Data Privacy" section in the privacy settings, you can review and adjust these preferences to align with your privacy concerns.

It's important to regularly review and update your privacy settings on LinkedIn, especially when there are changes to the platform's features or policies. By managing your privacy effectively, you can protect your professional information and engage with the LinkedIn community in a way that aligns with your personal preferences and goals.

8.2 Handling Endorsements and Recommendations

Endorsements and recommendations are valuable features on LinkedIn that can enhance your professional profile and credibility. Let's explore how to effectively handle endorsements and recommendations on LinkedIn.

Endorsements:

- Be strategic: Prioritize endorsements that align with your skills and expertise. Accept endorsements from individuals who can genuinely vouch for your abilities.

- Give to receive: Actively endorse your connections' skills. This can prompt them to reciprocate and endorse your skills in return.

- Customize your skills section: Arrange your skills in order of importance and relevance to your current professional goals. Focus on showcasing the skills you want to be endorsed for.

- Engage with your network: Regularly engage with your connections by sharing valuable content, participating in

- discussions, and providing meaningful feedback. This can encourage them to endorse your skills organically.

- Request targeted endorsements: Reach out to specific individuals in your network who have firsthand experience working with you and kindly request endorsements for specific skills. Personalize your message and explain how their endorsement would be beneficial.

Recommendations:

- Choose the right recommenders: Seek recommendations from colleagues, supervisors, clients, or mentors who can provide genuine insights into your professional capabilities. Aim for a diverse range of recommenders to showcase different aspects of your skills and character.

- Be specific in your requests: When asking for a recommendation, provide context by highlighting the specific projects, achievements, or skills you would like them to mention. This helps them craft a more tailored and impactful recommendation.

- Follow up and express gratitude: Once you receive a recommendation, take the time to thank the recommender. A thoughtful message of appreciation goes a long way and strengthens your professional relationships.

- Showcase recommendations strategically: Feature the most relevant and impressive recommendations prominently on your profile. LinkedIn allows you to reorder and highlight recommendations, so choose ones that align with your career objectives.

- Proactively offer recommendations: Be proactive in recommending others in your network who deserve it. This can prompt them to reciprocate and write recommendations for you as well.

Remember, endorsements and recommendations should reflect your true abilities and professional character. It's essential to maintain authenticity and integrity throughout the process. Regularly update and refresh your profile to ensure it accurately represents your current skills and achievements.

8.3 Dealing with negative feedback or criticism

Dealing with negative feedback or criticism on LinkedIn can be challenging, but it's an opportunity for growth and improvement.

Here are some key strategies to effectively handle negative feedback on the platform:

★ **Stay calm and composed**: It's natural to feel defensive or upset when receiving negative feedback, but it's crucial to remain calm and composed. Take a step back, breathe, and avoid responding impulsively. Give yourself time to process the feedback before formulating a thoughtful response.

★ **Evaluate the feedback objectively**: Assess the feedback objectively to determine its validity. Consider the source of the criticism, the specific points raised, and whether there is any merit to their concerns. Constructive feedback can provide valuable insights and help you enhance your professional reputation.

★ **Respond professionally**: When responding to negative feedback, maintain a professional tone and avoid becoming defensive or argumentative. Thank the person for their feedback and address their concerns thoughtfully. Demonstrate your willingness to listen, learn, and improve based on their input.

★ **Seek clarification**: If the feedback is unclear or lacks specific details, politely ask for clarification to gain a better understanding of the person's perspective. This shows your commitment to resolving the issue and can lead to a more productive conversation.

★ **Apologize when necessary**: If you made a mistake or if the feedback is warranted, offer a sincere apology. Taking responsibility for any errors or missteps demonstrates accountability and a willingness to make amends.

★ **Learn from the feedback**: Negative feedback can be an opportunity for self-improvement. Analyze the feedback to identify areas where you can enhance your skills, knowledge, or approach. Use it as a chance to grow and develop professionally.

★ **Engage in constructive dialogue**: Encourage a constructive conversation by inviting the person to further discuss their concerns or suggestions privately. This demonstrates your commitment to addressing the issue and finding a resolution. Engaging in a meaningful dialogue can also help clarify misunderstandings and foster a more positive relationship.

★ **Implement necessary changes**: If the feedback highlights valid points, take action to implement the necessary changes or improvements. Communicate these changes transparently, either through direct messages to the person who provided the feedback or by sharing updates publicly on your LinkedIn profile or relevant posts.

★ **Focus on positive interactions**: While negative feedback can be disheartening, remember that it's just one aspect of your professional journey. Shift your attention to the positive interactions and feedback you receive on LinkedIn. Engage with supportive connections, share valuable content, and build relationships based on trust and mutual respect.

★ **Learn to differentiate constructive criticism from trolling**: In some cases, negative feedback may be unfounded, irrelevant, or even malicious. Learn to distinguish between constructive criticism and trolling or personal attacks. If you encounter harassment or abusive behavior, report and block the individuals involved to maintain a safe and positive LinkedIn environment.

Remember, handling negative feedback effectively showcases your professionalism, adaptability, and commitment to growth. Utilize these strategies to turn negative experiences into opportunities for improvement and personal development on LinkedIn.

8.4 Keeping your profile up to date

Keeping your LinkedIn profile up to date is crucial for maximizing your professional visibility and opportunities. By regularly maintaining and enhancing your profile, you can effectively showcase your skills, experience, and accomplishments to potential employers, clients, and connections.

Here are some key steps to help you keep your profile up to date:

★ Update your headline and summary: Your headline and summary are the first things people see on your profile. Craft a compelling headline that accurately reflects your current role or professional goals. In the summary section, highlight your key achievements, skills, and aspirations, and make sure to keep it fresh by periodically adding new accomplishments.

★ Revise your work experience: Regularly review and update your work experience section to include your current and past positions, responsibilities, and accomplishments. Use concise and action-oriented language to describe your achievements and quantify results wherever possible. Include relevant keywords to improve your profile's searchability.

★ Showcase your skills: Skills are an important aspect of your LinkedIn profile. Ensure that your skills section accurately represents your current skill set and expertise. Add new skills as you acquire them and remove outdated or less relevant skills. Seek endorsements from colleagues and supervisors to validate your skills.

★ Incorporate multimedia elements: LinkedIn allows you to enhance your profile by adding multimedia elements such as documents, presentations, images, and videos. Take advantage of this feature to showcase your work samples, projects, or presentations to provide a more comprehensive view of your capabilities.

★ Request recommendations: Recommendations from colleagues, supervisors, and clients add credibility to your profile. Reach out to individuals you have worked closely with and ask them to provide a recommendation highlighting your skills, work ethic, and accomplishments. Offer to reciprocate by providing recommendations for others as well.

★ Engage with content: Actively engage with your network by sharing relevant industry articles, commenting on posts, and participating in discussions.

This demonstrates your knowledge and engagement in your field and helps build your professional reputation.

★ Update your contact information: Ensure that your contact information, such as email address and phone number, is accurate and up to date. This makes it easier for others to reach out to you and explore potential opportunities.

★ Stay active: Regularly log in to LinkedIn and stay active on the platform. This can involve connecting with new professionals, joining relevant groups and communities, and participating in LinkedIn's features, such as LinkedIn Live or LinkedIn Events. Active engagement increases your visibility and expands your professional network.

★ Monitor and respond to messages: Check your LinkedIn messages regularly and promptly respond to inquiries or connection requests. Timely and professional communication helps build relationships and can lead to valuable opportunities.

★ Stay informed about industry trends: Stay up to date with the latest developments in your industry and incorporate relevant keywords, topics, or skills in your profile. Join relevant industry groups, follow influential thought leaders, and share or engage with content related to your field of expertise.

Remember, keeping your LinkedIn profile up to date is an ongoing process. Regularly review and refine your profile to reflect your current professional status and goals. By investing time in maintaining your profile, you can leverage LinkedIn's powerful network to enhance your career prospects and professional connections.

8.5 Maintaining an active and professional presence

Maintaining an active and professional presence on LinkedIn is crucial for building a strong personal brand, expanding your professional network, and attracting relevant career opportunities.

Here are some key tips to help you maintain an active and professional presence on LinkedIn:

★ Complete your profile: Start by creating a comprehensive and well-structured profile. Include a professional headshot, write a compelling summary that highlights your skills and experiences, and provide detailed information about your work history, education, and certifications. Make sure to use relevant keywords to enhance your visibility in searches.

★ Engage regularly: Actively engage with your network by regularly posting and sharing relevant content. Share articles, industry news, or insights that demonstrate your expertise and interests. Additionally, comment on and like posts from others in your network to foster meaningful interactions.

★ Join relevant groups: Participate in LinkedIn groups related to your industry, professional interests, or areas of expertise. Engage in discussions, share insights, and connect with other professionals who share similar interests. This can help expand your network and establish your credibility within your field.

★ Build meaningful connections: Connect with professionals you know and trust, such as colleagues, clients, mentors, or classmates. When sending connection requests, personalize your message and explain why you want to connect. This personal touch can significantly increase the chances of your request being accepted.

★ Request and provide recommendations: Recommendations are valuable testimonials that enhance your professional credibility. Reach out to colleagues, clients, or supervisors and kindly request them to write a recommendation highlighting your skills, achievements, and work ethic. In turn, offer to write recommendations for others in your network as well.

★ Share your achievements: Celebrate your professional milestones, such as promotions, certifications, or project completions, by sharing them as updates or articles on LinkedIn.

This not only showcases your accomplishments but also reinforces your expertise and commitment to professional growth.

★ Network strategically: Leverage LinkedIn's search and advanced search features to find professionals in your industry or target companies. Connect with individuals who can offer valuable insights, mentorship, or potential job opportunities. Personalize your connection requests and follow up with a thoughtful message to nurture those connections.

★ Participate in LinkedIn's features: Stay up-to-date with LinkedIn's latest features and utilize them to enhance your presence. This includes posting videos, creating articles on LinkedIn Publishing, sharing presentations on SlideShare, or engaging in live events and webinars. Experiment with different formats to showcase your expertise and engage with your audience.

★ Monitor and manage your online presence: Regularly review and update your profile to reflect any changes in your professional journey. Keep your information accurate and ensure consistency across your online presence.

Additionally, monitor your privacy settings and manage notifications to control the visibility and frequency of updates from your network.

★ Be professional and respectful: LinkedIn is a professional platform, so maintain a professional tone in your communications and interactions. Be respectful and considerate when engaging with others, even if you have differing opinions. Building a positive and professional reputation on LinkedIn requires treating others with respect and courtesy.

By following these tips, you can establish and maintain an active and professional presence on LinkedIn, positioning yourself as a knowledgeable and engaged professional in your field and opening doors to new opportunities. Remember to be consistent, genuine, and proactive in your efforts to maximize the benefits of this powerful platform.

Chapter 9: Tips for LinkedIn Success

9.1 Dos and don'ts for LinkedIn beginners

Here are the key points to keep in mind:

Dos:

- Complete your profile: Fill out all the sections of your profile, including your headline, summary, experience, education, and skills. A complete profile enhances your professional credibility.

- Use a professional profile photo: Select a high-quality photo where you appear approachable and professional. Avoid using casual or cropped images.

- Craft a compelling headline: Your headline should go beyond just stating your job title. Highlight your unique skills, achievements, or areas of expertise to grab attention.

- Write a concise and impactful summary: Use this section to showcase your professional brand and career aspirations.

  Focus on your key skills, accomplishments, and what you can offer to potential connections.

- Customize your URL: Personalize your LinkedIn URL to make it more professional and easier to share. Ideally, use your name or a variation of it.

- Connect with others: Expand your network by connecting with colleagues, classmates, industry professionals, and other relevant contacts. Personalize connection requests to establish a genuine connection.

- Engage with content: Like, comment, and share posts that are relevant to your industry or interests. Engaging with others' content helps you build relationships and gain visibility.

- Join and participate in groups: Find and join LinkedIn groups related to your professional interests. Engage in discussions, share insights, and contribute valuable information to establish yourself as a knowledgeable professional.

- Share your own content: Create and share original articles, posts, or industry-related updates. Position yourself as a thought leader by providing valuable insights and expertise.

- Request and provide recommendations: Seek recommendations from colleagues, managers, or clients who can vouch for your skills and work. Additionally, offer recommendations to others when you genuinely appreciate their work.

Don'ts:

- Avoid excessive self-promotion: While it's important to showcase your skills and achievements, avoid constant self-promotion. Focus on providing value and building relationships rather than solely promoting yourself.

- Don't send generic connection requests: Personalize your connection requests to explain why you want to connect with someone. Generic requests without context may be perceived as spam.

- Refrain from controversial or unprofessional content: LinkedIn is a professional platform, so avoid sharing controversial opinions, offensive content, or anything that could damage your professional reputation.

- Don't ignore messages or connection requests: Be responsive to messages and connection requests in a timely manner. Ignoring or delaying responses can reflect poorly on your professionalism.

- Avoid excessive automation or bulk messaging: While tools can be helpful, excessive use of automation or sending generic bulk messages can come across as impersonal and spammy. Personalization is key.

- Don't overdo endorsements or ask for them excessively: Endorsements can validate your skills, but avoid endorsing people you don't know well or requesting endorsements from everyone you're connected with. Be selective and genuine.

- Refrain from overloading with irrelevant content: Share content that is relevant to your professional goals and industry. Avoid overloading your connections' feeds with unrelated or trivial information.

- Don't neglect your profile: Regularly update your profile to reflect your current skills, experiences, and achievements. An outdated profile may give the impression of disinterest or lack of activity.

- Avoid connecting with everyone indiscriminately: While growing your network is important, focus on quality over quantity. Connect with individuals who align with your professional goals and can add value to your network.

- Don't underestimate the power of privacy settings: Review and adjust your privacy settings based on your preferences. Be mindful of what information you share publicly and consider restricting access to sensitive

9.2 Strategies for building meaningful connections

Building meaningful connections on LinkedIn is essential for expanding your professional network, fostering collaborations, and opening up new opportunities.

Here are some strategies to help you build meaningful connections on LinkedIn:

★ Optimize Your Profile: Start by creating a compelling and professional LinkedIn profile. Use a high-quality profile picture, write a concise and engaging headline, and craft a compelling summary that highlights your skills and expertise. Make sure to include relevant keywords that reflect your professional interests and industry.

★ Define Your Networking Goals: Before reaching out to others, define your networking goals. Determine the types of connections you want to make, whether it's industry peers, potential clients, or mentors. Having a clear goal in mind will help you focus your efforts and connect with the right people.

★ Personalize Connection Requests: Avoid using generic connection requests and take the time to personalize each invitation. Mention why you are interested in connecting with the person, highlight common interests or mutual connections, and explain how you can potentially add value to their network.

★ Engage with Content: Actively engage with relevant content on LinkedIn by liking, commenting, and sharing posts. Share insightful thoughts, ask thoughtful questions, and contribute valuable information. By engaging with others' content, you can grab their attention and initiate meaningful conversations.

★ Join and Participate in Groups: LinkedIn Groups provide excellent opportunities to connect with like-minded professionals and engage in industry-specific discussions. Identify and join relevant groups within your industry or areas of interest. Contribute meaningfully to discussions, offer insights, and connect with individuals who share your professional passions.

★ Leverage Advanced Search: Utilize LinkedIn's advanced search feature to find professionals or companies in your target industry. Refine your search based on specific criteria such as location, industry, job title, or company size.

This enables you to identify individuals or organizations that align with your networking goals.

★ Request Introductions: Utilize your existing connections on LinkedIn to request introductions to individuals you want to connect with. Leverage mutual connections or reach out to someone you know well and ask for an introduction. This can help establish an initial level of trust and increase the likelihood of a meaningful connection.

★ Offer Value: Building meaningful connections is a two-way street. Look for ways to provide value to your connections. Share relevant industry insights, offer assistance, or provide introductions to others in your network. By demonstrating your willingness to contribute and help others, you can strengthen your relationships.

★ Attend Events and Webinars: Keep an eye out for virtual or in-person events, conferences, and webinars within your industry.

Participate actively, engage with speakers and attendees, and connect with individuals you meet during these events. This provides an excellent opportunity to establish new connections and deepen existing ones.

★ Follow Up and Nurture Relationships: Once you've made a new connection, don't forget to follow up and nurture the relationship. Send a personalized message expressing your gratitude for connecting, and find ways to stay engaged. Share relevant content, congratulate them on their achievements, or offer your assistance when appropriate.

Remember, building meaningful connections on LinkedIn requires time, effort, and authenticity. Focus on developing genuine relationships, providing value, and actively engaging with others, and you'll be able to create a strong and valuable professional network.

9.3 How to stand out in a competitive job market

To stand out in a competitive job market, it's crucial to strategically position yourself and showcase your unique value proposition. Here are several key strategies you can employ on LinkedIn to enhance your professional visibility and increase your chances of standing out:

★ Optimize your LinkedIn profile: Your profile is your online resume. Make sure it's complete, up-to-date, and engaging. Use a professional headshot, craft a compelling headline, and write a concise and impactful summary. Highlight your relevant skills, experience, and achievements.

★ Build a strong professional network: Connect with industry professionals, colleagues, mentors, and others who can add value to your network. Engage with their content, participate in relevant groups, and attend industry events to expand your connections.

★ Showcase your expertise: Share valuable content, articles, or industry insights on LinkedIn. Regularly post updates, articles, or videos to demonstrate your knowledge and expertise. Engage with others' content by commenting, liking, and sharing to increase your visibility and build credibility.

★ Obtain recommendations and endorsements: Request recommendations from colleagues, supervisors, or clients who can vouch for your skills and work ethic. Endorse others for their skills, and they may reciprocate. These endorsements and recommendations serve as social proof of your capabilities.

★ Join relevant LinkedIn groups: Engage in groups related to your industry or profession. Contribute to discussions, ask thoughtful questions, and provide valuable insights. This allows you to connect with like-minded professionals, stay updated on industry trends, and expand your visibility.

★ Actively search and apply for jobs: Utilize LinkedIn's job search feature to find opportunities that align with your skills and interests. Tailor your applications and resumes for each job, highlighting your relevant qualifications and achievements. Leverage your network to discover hidden job opportunities and ask for referrals.

★ Remember, actively search and apply for relevant job openings on LinkedIn. Follow and engage with companies you're interested in working for to stay updated on their news, updates, and job postings.

★ Engage with recruiters: Connect with recruiters specializing in your field. Engage with their posts, comment on job listings, and express your interest in relevant positions. Building relationships with recruiters can increase your chances of being considered for job opportunities.

★ Utilize LinkedIn features: Take advantage of LinkedIn's features to stand out. Publish articles on LinkedIn Pulse, share presentations or portfolio samples on SlideShare, and showcase your projects or work samples in the featured section of your profile. Consider using a customized LinkedIn URL to enhance your personal branding.

★ Continuously learn and develop: Showcase your commitment to professional growth by participating in online courses, certifications, or attending webinars. Update your skills and expertise on your profile and share your learning experiences with your network.

★ Engage in meaningful conversations: Be active in discussions related to your industry or profession. Provide thoughtful comments, ask questions, and share insights. Engaging in meaningful conversations helps you establish yourself as a thought leader and expand your network.

Remember, consistency and authenticity are key. Regularly update your profile, engage with others, and stay active on LinkedIn to maintain visibility and increase your chances of standing out in the competitive job market.

9.4 Maximizing the value of your LinkedIn network

To maximize the value of your LinkedIn network, follow these key strategies:

* ★ Optimize Your Profile: Create a compelling and professional profile that showcases your skills, experience, and achievements. Use a high-quality profile picture, write a compelling headline and summary, and include relevant keywords to enhance your visibility in searches.

* ★ Expand Your Network: Connect with professionals in your industry, colleagues, former classmates, and others who share

similar interests. Personalize your connection requests to establish a genuine connection and explain why you'd like to connect.

★ Engage Actively: Actively engage with your network by liking, commenting, and sharing relevant content. This helps you stay visible and build relationships with your connections. Join relevant LinkedIn groups and participate in discussions to expand your reach and demonstrate your expertise.

★ Share Valuable Content: Share informative and engaging content regularly to establish yourself as a thought leader. Post articles, industry insights, case studies, and helpful tips to provide value to your network. Use multimedia formats like images and videos to make your content more engaging.

★ **Utilize LinkedIn Publishing**: Leverage LinkedIn's publishing platform to write and share long-form articles on topics relevant to your industry. Publishing articles can help you showcase your expertise, gain visibility, and attract followers.

★ Request and Provide Recommendations: Request recommendations from colleagues, clients, and partners to enhance your credibility. Similarly, provide recommendations for others you have worked with to strengthen your professional relationships.

★ **Utilize Advanced Search**: Utilize LinkedIn's advanced search features to find professionals, companies, and opportunities aligned with your goals. Refine your searches by industry, location, job title, and other relevant criteria to identify valuable connections and potential leads.

★ Participate in LinkedIn Events: Attend virtual events, webinars, and workshops hosted on LinkedIn. Engage in discussions, ask questions, and network with participants to expand your network and gain industry insights.

★ **Utilize LinkedIn Analytics**: LinkedIn provides analytics on your profile views, post reach, and engagement metrics. Use this data to assess the effectiveness of your networking efforts, identify trends, and adjust your strategy accordingly.

★ Personalize Messages and Invitations: When reaching out to new connections or responding to messages, personalize your interactions. Take the time to understand their background, interests, and needs, and tailor your messages accordingly.

Chapter 10: Conclusion

Unlocking LinkedIn's potential is crucial for individuals aiming to excel in today's competitive job market. By harnessing the power of LinkedIn's extensive network, you can expand your professional reach, establish thought leadership, and build valuable connections. Leveraging the platform's features, such as optimizing profiles, engaging with relevant content, and utilizing advanced search filters, individuals can enhance their visibility, credibility, and career opportunities. Furthermore, embracing LinkedIn as a content creator enables professionals to share insights, showcase expertise, and nurture professional relationships. To maximize the benefits of LinkedIn, consistency, authenticity, and strategic networking are key. By investing time and effort into cultivating a strong LinkedIn presence, professionals can unlock a wealth of opportunities and open doors to new professional horizons. So, take action today, unlock your LinkedIn potential, and pave the way to a successful and fulfilling professional journey.

Taking your LinkedIn journey to the next level

Taking your LinkedIn journey to the next level requires a strategic approach and consistent effort. By implementing the key practices discussed in this book, you can unlock the full potential of LinkedIn and leverage it to advance your professional goals.

First and foremost, optimize your LinkedIn profile by using a professional headshot, crafting a compelling headline, and creating a concise yet impactful summary. Highlight your achievements, skills, and experiences to establish credibility and attract the attention of potential connections and employers.

Actively engage with the LinkedIn community by joining relevant groups, participating in discussions, and sharing valuable content. This will not only help you expand your network but also position yourself as a thought leader in your industry. Don't hesitate to contribute meaningful comments and offer insights to showcase your expertise and build relationships with fellow professionals.

Consistency is key when it comes to posting content on LinkedIn. Develop a content strategy that aligns with your personal brand and objectives. Regularly share original articles, industry news, thought-provoking questions, and valuable insights to demonstrate your knowledge and expertise. Engage with your audience by responding to comments and messages promptly, fostering meaningful connections.

Utilize the power of LinkedIn's advanced search and connection features to expand your network strategically. Seek out professionals in your field, potential mentors, industry influencers, and individuals who share your interests. Personalize your connection requests and engage in meaningful conversations to nurture relationships.

Leverage the LinkedIn publishing platform to showcase your expertise and thought leadership. Write and publish articles on topics relevant to your industry, providing valuable insights and solutions to common challenges. By consistently delivering high-quality content, you can attract a larger audience and establish yourself as a trusted authority.

Lastly, don't underestimate the importance of continuous learning and professional development. Stay updated on industry trends and advancements by following influential thought leaders and joining relevant LinkedIn groups. Participate in webinars, workshops, and online courses to enhance your skills and expand your knowledge base.

Overall, taking your LinkedIn journey to the next level requires a proactive approach, consistent effort, and a genuine desire to build meaningful connections. By optimizing your profile, engaging with the community, sharing valuable content, expanding your network strategically, showcasing your expertise through publishing, and investing in continuous learning, you can unlock the full potential of LinkedIn and accelerate your professional growth.

Remember, LinkedIn is not just a platform for job seekers; it's a powerful tool for building a strong professional brand and connecting with opportunities that can propel your career forward. So, embrace the possibilities, stay authentic, and watch your LinkedIn journey soar to new heights.